What Every Landlord
Needs to Know

What Every Landlord Needs to Know

Time and Money-Saving Solutions to Your Most Annoying Problems

Richard H. Jorgensen

McGraw-Hill

New York Chicago San Francisco Lisbon London
Madrid Mexico City Milan New Delhi San Juan
Seoul Singapore Sydney Toronto

This publication is designed to provide accurate and authoritative information in regard to the subject matter covered. It is sold with the understanding that neither the author nor the publisher is engaged in rendering legal, accounting, or other professional service. If legal advice or other expert assistance is required, the services of a competent professional person should be sought.
—*From a Declaration of Principles jointly adopted by a Committee of the American Bar Association and a Committee of Publishers*

McGraw-Hill books are available at special quantity discounts to use as premiums and sales promotions, or for use in corporate training programs. For more information, please write to the Director of Special Sales, McGraw-Hill Professional, Two Penn Plaza, New York, NY 10121-2298. Or contact your local bookstore.

 This book is printed on recycled, acid-free paper containing a minimum of 50% recycled de-inked fiber.

Contents

Chapter 1

Selecting High-Quality Tenants

Marketing Your Product

The key to a successful and profitable real estate investment business is selecting the best tenants possible. And one of the key elements in selecting and attracting the best tenants is to *market your rental unit so the ideal tenants like what they see*. As you begin the search for the best tenants, the number-one concern for you should be this: Start with what *you* have to offer. In other words, get *your* "house" in order.

Solution

Here's a 10-Step Program on How to Get Your House in Order

Step Number 1: At all times, before making arrangements to show the rental unit to a potential tenant, take the time to thoroughly scrutinize the rental unit yourself. Look it over. Ask yourself, "Is this a place where I'd consider living?"

As they inspect the apartment, most people will be looking for obvious deficiencies. They want to know if the various utilities, stove, refrigerator, dishwasher, and hot water heater are in good working order. The good tenants you're seeking aren't dumb, so you can be assured that they are going to be very observant of whether the unit is clean.

As you go through your building, check the basement. Make sure it's not full of leftover junk from previous tenants. I've gone into some basements and found a collection of clutter consisting of old mattresses, davenports, chairs, and many other items.

Once you've completed your inspection and you're ready for the showing, go through the unit and review your property and ask yourself, "Am I satisfied that everything is in tip-top shape and ready to show?"

Step Number 2: *Check the fire extinguishers, smoke detectors, and smoke alarms.* I highlight and magnify this item, fire-related equipment, because of its importance. Make sure that all of the fire safety equipment is in proper working order.

Here's something many landlords overlook. Smoke detectors and smoke alarms have a limited life span. If you have any question about the length of time they've been in your unit, don't hesi-

tate to buy and install new fire and safety equipment at regular intervals. It's inexpensive insurance.

Periodically ask the tenant to check and make sure the smoke alarm and fire extinguisher are working and in proper order. If you have a feeling that the tenant might not do this, then take it upon yourself to check them.

In fact, I'd make it a point to personally take the time to inspect the fire extinguisher. There's an indicator that shows if it's in proper working order and whether it is fully charged. If it's not at full charge, have it recharged.

If the fire extinguisher is located inside of a cabinet or cupboard, purchase a red warning sticker that says "FIRE EXTHINGUSHER INSIDE." Place this sticker on the outside of the cupboard door.

I don't think it's a sound idea to buy and install the least expensive fire prevention equipment. If a fire should occur, and it's discovered that you installed a "cheap" fire alarm or detector, an attorney will focus on this detail and might be able to use it against you.

If your building has natural gas heat and gas appliances, stove, and gas dryer, install a carbon monoxide detector. As with your fire protection equipment, this also can be inexpensive insurance. Here's a case to illustrate why you must have all this equipment working properly and in first-class condition.

My friend, the owner of a sixplex, rented one of the units to a single working woman. She checked out well in the application for rent and the credit report. One evening she returned to her apartment and started preparing her meal on an electric stove. She left the kitchen, went into the living room to watch the news, and fell asleep. The stove burner remained on while the food was cooking; well, let's say it overcooked. Eventually, with no one watching, something ignited and started a fire. The smoke awakened her. As she woke up, she discovered flames in the cooking pan and all over the burner.

She didn't have a working fire extinguisher available, so, in a state of panic, she quickly grabbed the food pan by the hand and put it in the sink, ran water over it and put out the flame. By then the kitchen was filled with smoke. She called the fire department and fortunately they used a chemical rather than water to douse the flame. After everything was doused there was considerable smoke damage throughout the apartment. This included burned and scorched woodwork around the countertop, and the stove itself was ruined.

My friend, the owner of the building, filed a claim with his insurance company. There was no problem with the claim, and basically few questions were asked by the adjustor. The insurance company covered the fire loss in the apartment.

But what made this an unusual story was that as she picked up the pan that she put it in the sink, she suffered severe burns to her hands. She went to the hospital for treatment, and the cost was $500. Even though she was completely at fault, the landlord's insurance company paid the $500 hospital bill.

The owner was out a couple of months' rent because the fire damage throughout the apartment rendered it unusable, because it needed a considerable amount of repair and replacement. He, unfortunately, didn't have insurance coverage for the rent loss.

The landlord asked his insurance adjuster about the $500 hospital bill, "Why should we be responsible for her carelessness?" The adjuster simply said, "It's less expensive to pay this small claim rather than getting involved with any legal action. He said, "Once an attorney enters the picture, the cost doubles and triples,

and you never know what we could end up with, loss of work time, psychological trauma, inability to have children. Who knows what all?"

I'm sure there are hundreds of stories about fires that occurred when the smoke detectors, fire alarms, or fire extinguishers didn't work or weren't available. Therefore, do whatever it takes and everything within your means to keep that property from being vulnerable to any kind of lawsuit.

Step Number 3: The next important inspection should be the kitchen. Check the floors, window coverings, curtains, blinds, or drapes for stains, dirt, and grease. Make sure the refrigerator is clean and in prime condition. Does the dishwasher smell from the previous tenant's use, and is it clean?

Are the stove and air vents clean? Are there cracks and crevices on the stove filled with cooking grease from the previous tenant?

How are the kitchen cupboards? Think of this. Tenants are placing all of their personal eating utensils, probably a lot of them wedding gifts, into that cupboard. I'm sure you can understand that no one wants to see dirt, spider webs, or, worse than anything, mouse droppings in the cupboards.

The kitchen and bathroom are two prime areas that you want to present to the new tenant as being meticulously clean.

Step Number 4. How does the all-important bathroom look? Would you have second thoughts about using the bathroom if you lived there? If so, correct whatever you observe, smell, or find objectionable. Is it clean? Does it *smell* good? Is the shower or bathtub clean? A new toilet seat is a simple and inexpensive improvement. There's nothing that will turn off anyone more than an ugly, cracked, or dirty toilet seat. Put in a new roll of toilet paper.

Step Number 5: Don't hesitate to use a good-smelling soap or cleaning agent. If the unit smells fresh and clean, it's to your benefit. Maybe it's best to avoid Lysol. Another smell that is distasteful is roach spray.

Step Number 6: Are any of the rooms in need of painting? Are the carpets clean?

Step Number 7: The entire unit should be in tip-top shape. If it's not, the odds are pretty good that you're going to have a crummy-looking rental unit and you're going to end up with a crummy tenant. It's that simple.

Step Number 8: Everything should be in excellent condition so that when you're showing, you won't be embarrassed or have to make excuses or apologize about dirt or clutter, or whatever that can be distracting in the eyes of that potential tenant. *Make certain that you never get branded as a "slum landlord."*

Step Number 9: Now you should be ready for the all-important showing. If you know and feel that your unit is ready, make sure you accompany the potential tenant.

Step Number 10: Allow the tenants to have a private look on their own. Once the one-on-one showing is completed, here's an idea I've used that has worked wonderfully well for me.

Once I've determined that this potential tenant is a good choice, and I like what I see, I make a mental commitment. When I've finished the tour of the premises with the tenants, I tell them, "I'm going to leave you now and you can spend some time in the apartment. This will be your home and I want to be sure you're satisfied. By spending a little time alone here, this can give you an idea of what kind of a home you can make for yourself."

I then add, "I'll be back in about a half-hour and then you can give me your decision."

On the other hand, if I have any sense that that individual just doesn't "click" with me, I rush through the showing and say, "I'll get back to you because I have others who are waiting to see the unit. As soon as the showing is over, I'll call you." I always have a backup with someone to call once this interview is concluded. That usually ends it.

Now let's see who those renters are that are considered the best.

Chapter 2

Finding the Ideal Tenant

Who Are the Best Tenants?

If you select only the best tenants, you will eliminate many other problems. This can include general upkeep of the rental unit, receiving rent on time, and just plain getting along well with the tenant. In other words establishing a good tenant-landlord relationship.

You probably already know this, but it bears repeating. There are some people who, for one reason or another, simply don't care to own their home. I suspect these people prefer living in an apartment or a rental unit so they don't have to be bothered with mowing the grass, shoveling snow in the winter months, or tending to the various maintenance issues with home ownership. And a renter has no mortgage payment. Those of us who are homeowners can certainly understand that.

And, of course, there are some people who simply can't afford to own a home. That means there are and always will be certain numbers of people who are available to rent an apartment. How do we find those people and make sure we get the right ones?

I've got to admit it's fairly easy for me to say, "select only the best tenants." Everyone would like to do that. But that job, as a landlord, is not as simple as it might sound. I'm thoroughly convinced that it takes time and work to select the best. And let me add, the more screening you do, the better the tenant.

Just as important, make sure you don't end up with an undesirable tenant. We'll discuss the undesirable tenants and what this can lead to more thoroughly as we go through this text.

I know some landlords who just don't take the time, and they often end up with the "slugs." That, of course, is their business. I say, "Let them have the 'questionable' tenants."

Profile of the Ideal Tenant

From my years of experience in the rental business, I've been able to compose a list of individuals or couples that I consider very acceptable and desirable as tenants. However, don't totally rely on this list as your final decision. Depend more on the application for rent or lease, your personal interview, and that all-important credit report.

There is no secret list of good, better, or best tenants that I know of. I'm not sure that my list is adequate, and I know it's not complete. But at least it's a guide that can be a starter for you to consider as a potential investor or present landlord.

Now, let's get on with finding a list of potential best tenants.

Professional and Semiprofessional Medical Service People

I personally have always had good experience and have rated high on my list the following:

- Licensed practical nurses
- Registered nurses

- X-ray technicians
- Medical technicians
- Most health care personnel

On a couple of occasions I've had the opportunity to rent to a doctor (intern) who lived in our community. Most interns are single and look for a single-person apartment. This is usually good for, at the most, one or sometimes two years. As we all know, by the time the interns become full-fledged doctors, they can afford their own home, so the odds of getting a full-fledged doctor as a full-time tenant are minimal.

Educated, Intelligent, Considerate People

Most people working in the medical profession are fairly well educated and intelligent enough to understand that when they live in an apartment complex, they must be considerate of the other people living in the same building. The nice thing about this group is that almost all medical people make a decent salary, so they can easily afford the rent.

In general I can say, in my case, that they have always been neat and clean and take good care of their living quarters. When their lease is expired the apartment is left in usually good condition, and that means it doesn't take a great deal of cleaning and preparing for the next tenant. You can, naturally, expect some wear and tear, so it's not out of the question that you might have to do some work, but there shouldn't be any major overhauling.

Usually most of the above-mentioned tenants are single. Consequently they entertain conservatively. That's not to say you want to overlook married couples. By all means, they can also be A-1 tenants.

With this category of people, I've found that you most likely won't experience or deal with loud parties, loud music, or wild guests. These are irritants that you don't want to handle.

College Professors, College Staff Members, High-School Teachers

- Administrators and assistants
- Faculty members
- Clerks, office workers
- Food service personnel
- Teachers

Most educators are paid a good salary so they too can afford the rent. And as with medical professionals, college-educated people are sophisticated and know enough to realize that they live in an apartment environment.

However, there's one minor glitch for you to consider. Some highly educated people can sometimes become overbearing when it comes to demands or complaints. Some seem to have a tendency to see every little glitch or scar or problem in their living quarters or in the building. There often can be a multitude of complaints, such as the faucet leaks, the washer doesn't wash the clothing properly, the dryer doesn't dry, the refrigerator is too cold or not cold enough, or any other small problem. Most of the time they become insistent, and whenever they find a problem, they become demanding and require that whatever it is be taken care of right away.

Incidentally, here's a good time to tell you by all means put in coin-operated laundry equipment. The main complaint you'll receive regarding the washers and dryers is that the tenants overload them. They think they can save money.

Most landlords realize that these types of complaints are part of the life of a landlord, and live with it. In my opinion, if it's a good tenant, take care of the problem as quickly as possible. This will not only establish a good rapport with the tenant, but also it will enhance your reputation as a landlord. The word gets out, especially in smaller communities. Having a good reputation is a great referral system. You'll like to hear, "She's a good landlord and takes good care of her buildings and tenants."

Mature Single or Married People

- Mature elderly tenants
- Retirees
- Widows, widowers

I've always had great experience renting to and providing housing for "mature" older tenants. Here's a case in point. A middle-aged divorced woman moved into our community to be close to her children and grandchildren. She rented my apartment, where she remained as a top-notch tenant for nine years. I rarely had a complaint. She took care of everything, kept it cleaned, and fixed or had fixed whatever needed fixing. She installed and paid for new carpeting in her living room. The rent was paid the first of the month without question.

Do you know something? I only raised her rent one time in nine years, and in the long run I made more money from not raising the rent and not having to deal with vacancies for nine years. She was what I would call an A-1 tenant.

Also, some good tenants are retirees, older widows, and widowers who no longer want to take care of a personal home. I've found that usually, if they're satisfied with the management of the building and you take care of them, they remain in the apartment until they are forced to live in a nursing home or whatever their next phase of life is.

What I've found is that most of the retired men who become tenants will look after their own apartment, usually without complaints and fix it themselves. They will often take on various tasks in the entire apartment building, taking care of the property and for the most part do it for no extra pay. They're looking "for something to do." This is indeed a special aspect of renting to older men.

Individuals and/or Couples Who Are Gainfully Employed

- Newly married couples
- Individuals and couples gainfully employed

As you analyze their rental application make sure that the applicant or applicants are employed by a reliable and stable business firm.

I say this because there are many instances where companies move into a community, take advantage of the tax breaks until they're used up, and then move on to another community and fleece them out of these same benefits. In our community we had just such an experience with PPG. They left our community after receiving and using up their tax benefits and moved on to another community. When they were here they hired a lot of people, filled most of the apartments, and every landlord flourished.

We also had an experience where a "big" corporation bought out a small business operation in our community. The "big" corporation moved part of its operation to its home base and then laid off some 130 employees. The community had many rental vacancies.

There's nothing more devastating to a community than when a corporation moves out or there's a consolidation of the corporation. It leaves a scar that often can be untreatable. When this happens, you can be sure that there will be an influx of apartment vacancies. So make sure, as you investigate your community for a site where you'd like to invest, that your tenants aren't subject to being laid off and subsequently won't have the income to pay the rent.

Government Office Employees

Most government employees have been well screened or they wouldn't be working for the government. This means, in the most part, they are reliable people.

Government-Subsidized Tenants

Be careful when I say government-subsidized tenants. I'm not talking here about welfare recipients. There are discrimination laws regarding rent policies for welfare recipients. Check your state laws. If not covered, you can be assured that if they're turned down for rent, you're going to attract the attention of legal aid services. So again, be careful.

However, here's the rental experience I had with two mentally disadvantaged men. Both of them were provided with government income. One man had the mental capability of maybe a 6 or 8 year old, the other maybe a 13 or 14 year old. They were both in their 30s. The "13-14" more or less looked after the "6-8." Both were physically in good health. For the most part they were able to take care of themselves, although a government-paid overseer came to their apartment daily to help them handle their business affairs.

In years past, most of these people were put in special homes where they had 24-hour assistance. In the l930s and 1940s, they spent their lives in mental institutions. We have made some progress.

It was discovered that some of these individuals could function quite well without 24-hour assistance if they were moved into normal neighborhoods in an average apartment. In my case of taking these two men in as tenants, it not only worked well, but outstandingly well.

Each of them had their own checkbooks and wrote their own checks for rent. Well, let's say they signed their checks as best they could. Usually the aid taking care of them would make out the check.

They did not have cooking privileges, so the stove was never used. This, of course eliminated any fear of fire. Neither of them smoked.

They both had menial government-subsidized jobs. For instance, they both worked at a local garage and a grocery store sweeping and cleaning floors. In addition to the pay they received, they were given a stipend from the government and they always had enough money to pay their rent and other expenses. I hired the "13-14" to mow the lawn and shovel winter snow.

They were extraordinarily clean. I say this because I have a coin-operated washer and dryer in the basement. From my coin count, I knew they were extra special clean because they were constantly washing and drying their clothing.

There were other tenants in my building, and never once did anyone else complain about these two men. In fact, most of them developed a friendship with the two.

They lived in my building for nine years. I sold the building and that was the end of my relationship with them. I've often said, to other apartment owners, that these two men turned out to be two of the best tenants I ever had in all the 30-plus years I owned rental property.

Gays, Lesbians, Unmarried Couples

Gays and lesbians have been some of my best tenants. I've also talked to other landlords, and they agree.

I only talked to one landlord who told me that he had a lady nurse tenant and she had a cat that was not taken care of. The cat odor was unbearable, and when she moved out the carpet had to be replaced and the entire unit had to be cleaned. You'd think that an intelligent, educated person would know better. Here's a case for having a "no pet" policy.

Most lesbians and gays I've known are outstandingly competent and usually very bright and intelligent, reliable people. For instance, I rented an apartment to a homosexual college professor. He was never overly demanding, paid his rent on time, and remained in the same apartment for 12 years. I can say without question that he was an outstanding tenant. My experience with lesbians and gays has been more than satisfactory.

I also have no problem recommending reliable (both employed) unmarried couples. However, only after conducting a credit check on *both* individuals. This recommendation does not include all unmarried male-female students living together unless they totally qualify. When I say qualify, I mean qualify. I'd give some consideration to upper-class students, juniors and seniors in college. There's more on students later.

I can tell you this: If I had to eliminate all the couples who weren't married, I'd have been faced with a lot of vacancies.

The moral of the story is, don't let your prejudices rule your real estate rental business life. It pays to use common sense.

Military Personnel

Most landlords who own property near military bases tell me that they have always had good experiences renting to noncommissioned and commissioned officers. Although military pay is dreadfully low, they usually are given a housing allowance. In addition, I've been told that if that military person does get behind on her rent you are allowed to contact her commanding officer, and that gets immediate results.

I have a friend who owns and manages 30 rental units located 15 miles from a major Air Force base. He told me that in all the years he's rented to military personnel, he's never had one bad experience. He did emphasize that if any problem occurred he would call the commanding officer and the problem would be taken care of immediately, no matter what it was.

I can understand this, because I know that military service is not a democracy but a hierarchy. The officer above you is always in charge and I mean in charge.

College Students

If you invest in a college community out of necessity, you will in all probability rent to college students. But picking "good" college students takes some finesse and tact. I start by telling you to be cautious. There are some college students who make good tenants.

THE PLIGHT OF FRESHMEN AND SOPHOMORES

I personally eliminate all freshmen, most sophomores, and many athletes. Do you know that only 33 percent of entering freshman graduate from college? For the first year those students are in college to party and raise hell. You can understand that because many freshmen have just been released from a repressive high school. In the college environment, they have no supervision and suddenly realize they can do whatever they want. However, good, mature juniors and seniors who are intent on getting a degree are comparatively good.

There's a section on some of the disadvantages of renting to college students. More on that later.

The Full Benefits of Referrals

One of the very best sources of good, reliable tenants is referrals from other tenants.

As a matter of fact, I know a landlord who has inserted the following statement in his lease:

We will add $25 to your rent deposit refund if you schedule an appointment with us for one of your friends if they become one of our tenants.

That statement could also be included in the moving-out contract.

Often a call would come from current tenants telling me they have a friend coming into town and asking if I have any vacancies.

In addition, when a current tenant gives 30-day notice that they are moving, and if it's a tenant that I've had a good relationship with, I ask them, "Do you have a friend or do you know anyone who would like to rent your apartment?" Many times I receive a positive response.

On many occasions I've had tenants come to me and say, "I've got a good friend who would like to take over my apartment. Is it all right?" This works and has been fruitful. I've used it a lot. Let me give you an example.

I had a single college professor who rented from me for five years. After five years she notified me that she had another job and was moving to another college community. She informed me early on that she had a good friend, a couple, who were moving into our community and becoming members of the faculty at the college. She had told her good friend that I was a good landlord. Subsequently the new couple came to me, and after the interview and credit check, I accepted them as tenants.

They have since become my good friends. An added benefit is that the husband, a computer whiz, has helped me with my computer problems. This has worked out extremely well.

As a matter of fact, that new tenant has been better than good. He, the husband of the faculty member, came to me and said he knew I was having some sewer problems. And I did. I had to call the plumber at least three times a year to clean out the tree roots, especially in the late spring and early summer of the year when the tree roots started infiltrating the sewer lines. He told me he found an acid type chemical that works in the sewer line and that he'd take care of the problem. He did, and since then I haven't had a problem nor have I had to call or need the services of a roto rooter. He has eliminated the sewer line problem in my building.

This method of seeking out good tenants through referrals has been very efficient.

Rich People

This section is solely for Donald Trump, probably one of the largest owners of luxury apartments in the country. I can imagine that you probably need a million dollars just to say hello. You can imagine how much he needs my advice on how to select and find the best tenants, but I'm giving it anyway.

It's simple. Select people with a lot of money. However, I don't know many rich people, and those I do know own their own apartments.

 **Solution**

Market Your Rental Business

Here are some ideas of how to market your rental business so you can be first in line to select the ideal tenants.

With my 30-plus years of experience in the rental business, in addition to talking to other property owners, I can pass on to you some reliable systems that have worked for me and other landlords in finding good tenants.

One of the first methods I found is this: I made contact with the personnel office at the college. Most colleges and universities have an ever-changing faculty and staff, which means for a landlord the expectation of annual, and ongoing change and new people moving in. As I established a reputation of being a good landlord, I frequently received calls from the college personnel office for a professor or an employee coming into the system.

Secondly, our community is the home office of a large multinational corporation. I contacted their personnel office and told them that I had apartment rentals. Again, my reputation as a good landlord worked for me and many calls came from this company.

Thirdly, I contacted the local medical offices. I notified the various personnel that they could count on me to have good, clean, reasonably priced apartments.

In addition, in the community itself as I established a reputation of being a reliable and good landlord, I received many unsolicited calls from various referrals. It was not unusual that I'd receive out-of-town calls from new employees before they even moved into our community.

All of this worked satisfactorily.

Seek Out Government-Subsidized Tenants

With the good experience I had with the two mentally disadvantaged men in my apartment, I called the government agency that oversees these people, and I would tell them when I had a vacancy. I usually got a positive response; they were always interested in examining the property I had. Most of the time they preferred housing that didn't have steps, so this was often a drawback. But it certainly turned out to be a good source of renters.

Maintain a Good Reputation

You'll realize that once you've established a good reputation as a landlord, often companies and offices in the community will call you and ask if you have any vacancies. They will also refer their new, incoming personnel to you. This can occur before running a vacancy ad in the newspaper.

I think it's important for me to add this. Those personal experiences all occurred in a smaller community. I have no experience in an urban, metropolitan area.

From these various successful experiences and benefits I've realized, I have no qualms about recommending investing in a smaller community. I doubt that you can build a "good" reputation as a landlord in a big city. I'll have more to tell you about this, urban versus rural investing, later.

Chapter 3

Screening Out
the Most Undesirable
Tenants

Legal Means of Screening Tenants

The U.S. Department of Housing and Urban Development doesn't provide a great deal of information or direction for landlords to follow in establishing their rights for refusal to rent. However, there is a three-page bulletin formulated and distributed by the U.S. Department of Housing and Urban Development. The bulletin primarily covers the rights of tenants. However, there is a short list covering landlords' rights on page three of the document. It indicates to me that government agencies don't give a great deal of consideration for the needs of the landlords despite the fact they expect landlords to provide housing for people.

Landlords' Rights

Here are the items listed on page three of this bulletin that very briefly explain the landlords' rights in screening applicants. Here is their list that they consider a right of refusal to rent:

- Ability to pay rent
- Credit history
- Rental history

But let me advise you, unequivocally, that there are indeed many more and very significant and legal means of disqualifying potential tenants that we're going to cover more thoroughly in this chapter.

The Art of Screening Tenants

Screening and acquiring good tenants for a real estate investor is an art within itself. However, screening out and avoiding and rejecting the undesirable tenants is as important as acquiring good tenants.

You might ask, "How do I know and how do I go about recognizing and screening the undesirable tenants? Who are they?"

I don't have all the answers, and you might learn of other methods that I haven't covered. However, you can start by using some of the following criteria to screen and eliminate the undesirable, trouble-causing tenants.

Any of the following list of undesirable potential tenants can create, for any landlord, overwhelming problems that you don't want to deal with or need in your business. You don't want these problems for two reasons: one, the profit of your business, and the other, which is just as important, your peace of mind.

Disclaimer

The following list is presented as a generic representation of potential tenants that is provided to the reader without prejudice.

Drugs and Drug-Related Problems

Let's start with the most damaging, distressing, and anxiety filled problems that some potential tenants can create. Drugs and drug use includes anyone involved with or who has had any association with any drug habit, self-inflicted drug usage, the sale of drugs, the manufacturing of drugs, or drug dealing of any kind, either on or off the premises.

Drug users and drug-infested property can cause a distressing and anxiety-filled experience of unbelievable proportions for a property owner. In addition to the anxiety that drug problems can create, there's the threat of damage to the reputation of the property. I can assure you that anyone who occupies your property and is a habitual drug user and/or drug dealer can and will create a nightmare for you.

Dealing with Tenants Who Use Drugs

Here are some real-life stories that have occurred with landlords and drug users and drug dealers. The following story tells how a minor drug problem turned into a disastrous experience.

I talked to this landlord and here's his story. He told me that he rented an apartment to an individual who had recently been released from a drug treatment center. Because of various discrimination laws, he was reluctant to decline renting to the individual out of the fear of being attacked by some government agency. Not only was there the fear of dealing with some bureaucrat, but there was also a fear of being sued for discrimination. And as we all know, there are some legal aid services everywhere and anywhere just waiting to take on cases like this, protecting the criminal, especially where they detect vulnerable, "rich" landlords.

Most government "legal aiders" consider landlords as fair game. Once they get on your case, they'll pester you until you either bend to them or go broke fighting them.

Although this particular landlord knew the tenant had a history of being on and off drugs, he also knew that when the tenant was off drugs he was not a disreputable person The fact is, off drugs he was very much a kind and considerate individual. My landlord friend said that when this individual was off drugs, he was in fact "honest and friendly." It is usually the case, if you know anyone on drugs, that these people, when sober, are pretty decent.

This particular "cured" drug addict told my friend the landlord that he'd never go back on drugs again. He said, "This will never happen again."

So, my friend said to me, "Out of kindness and trying to be a good human being and a good landlord, I rented to him."

That was the landlord's first mistake. History will tell you that with most habitual drug users, eventually they do "fall off the wagon" and get right back into their own habit. And that's what happened in this case. This person did go back on drugs.

The Cost of a Drug Habit

As everyone knows, drug use is costly. That means this so-called "don't worry because he'd never back on drugs again" spent all his money to support this disastrous habit.

This opened the door for nothing but grief for my friend the landlord. It's a pretty well known fact to anyone who's ever dealt with anyone on drugs that this scenario, taking in a "cured" drug user, will usually backfire and become an expensive experience. And it did for my friend.

The first thing that happened was my friend was confronted by his tenant, weeping and crying and asking for more time to pay his rent. And of course he didn't want to give up the security of his home. The next mistake my friend the landlord made was not being forceful enough and allowing the drug user to get behind on his rent.

So what happened? The next stage was the tenant did end up back in a treatment center. Now the landlord had a situation with no rental income and an apartment full of the tenants' personal belongings. This also meant there was no way to collect any past-due rent.

What could he do at this stage? Not much. He could go through the court system and procure an eviction notice. This is costly, and he'd have to pay all the court costs. Not only would it be costly, and in all likelihood fruitless, but time-consuming.

In addition there's a possibility that an overly protective bureaucracy of one kind or another is going to protect the drug user and might not allow eviction until the "second cure" takes place.

There's also, with various government agencies and bureaucracies, the ever-present possibility of a lawsuit. Frankly, with this kind of episode you can eventually find yourself, the landlord, ending up paying a hefty price. This can be a financial sinkhole.

How Dual Tenancy and Drugs Can Become a Problem

Here's another case of a landlord involved with tenants on drugs. This landlord, the owner of an eightplex apartment building, took in two young students who were employed sufficiently that between the two of them they could pay the rent. They both checked out satisfactorily, one actually better than the other, so he rented to them.

As time went on the "better one" moved out. When she moved out, her friend, the "not so good one," kept the apartment. She had her dear, sweet "boyfriend" in, without permission from the landlord, to cohabitat and share the expenses of the apartment.

The boyfriend turned out to be on drugs and a drug dealer. This was the beginning of a stack of trouble for the owner. First of all, cars started coming and going day and night. The owner received calls from the other tenants about the traffic coming and going, which, as you can imagine can be a very upsetting situation for the other tenants. They threatened to leave.

The owner made contact with the "not so good" tenant and her boyfriend. This didn't turn out very well because he was met with a great deal of hostility when he confronted them with the issue of "what's going on here." They implied that it was none of his business, that they were paying the rent and had a right to do as they pleased.

Well, that's all that was needed. The landlord didn't take that offensive treatment and simply informed the girl and her boyfriend to get out of the apartment and be out that day or he'd contact the police.

The landlord said, "I'm sure they didn't want anything to do with the police, knowing they had the drug situation, so they left."

However, the owner ended up with two months' rent-past due. He had a rent deposit to cover part of it, but it took this much and more to clean up the apartment after they left hurriedly. It was good riddance.

Hostility and Arrogance Take Over

One of the most distressing stories about a drug user was from a friend of mine, the owner of three sixplexes. Here's his story.

He said that he rented an apartment to a man and had no indication or suspicion whatsoever that he was personally using drugs. After the tenant settled in for a couple of months, my friend discovered that he was holding all-night drug parties in the apartment. That was when things started to unravel. The other five tenants in the building started calling and complaining and they too threatened to leave.

My friend, the landlord, confronted the drug tenant and told him that he wanted him out of the apartment building because he didn't allow drug use. The tenant became hostile and arrogant. My friend said that this guy knew his rights, and insisted that he, the landlord, follow the legal procedure to evict him and that he was not going to leave until he received an eviction notice.

In order to do so, my friend discovered he had to have $265 to start the execution through the court system. He knew that if he spent that kind of money, there would be no way to recover it from the drug user. He ended up contacting an attorney who sent a letter threatening to contact the legal officials and demanding immediate eviction. This got the tenant out.

Drug Houses and Drug Neighborhoods

A more devastating scenario for a property owner is that the property itself can acquire the reputation of being a chronic drug house or drug location. This can not only tag your property as a drug house, but also it can lead to a situation where the entire area is labeled a drug neighborhood. God only knows you don't need or want this to happen to your property, and I can assure you your neighbors don't either.

Once the drug syndrome is established on a property or in a neighborhood, the property itself gains an indefensible and unfavorable reputation. And reestablishing the property with a drug free reputation is nearly impossible.

A drug-contaminated property can become an almost insurmountable and intolerable problem to solve. A drug house can and will deteriorate and literally destroy the property to the point that it can become valueless.

Drug Laws Covering Landlords

It is necessary that you know and become totally familiar with the various laws covering drug-related incidents having to do with rental property. For instance, some states have laws that put the onus on the landlord. If, for instance, the house is raided and police find any activity regarding drugs occurring on your property, the responsibility is placed on the landlord to correct (clean up) the problem, whatever it might be. In some states there are laws where the government can actually confiscate drug property, despite the fact that the landlord had nothing to do with the drug problem.

 Solution to Drug Problems

It's simple for me to tell you to be totally aware of and avoid any individual or person involved with drugs, as a consumer or dealer. I'd like to give you a specific answer of how to avoid them and make sure you don't end up with a "druggie" as a tenant, but I can't. However, there are some suggestions and steps you can take that can provide some protection.

First of all, I'm convinced that a credit report will help and can reveal some of the character flaws of an individual. So don't hesitate to start with the credit report.

If you're not sure, before you make a commitment to rent, and you have some suspicious about the person, check the public records at the county Clerk of Court office. These records, and they are public records that you have every right to, will reveal criminal activities and any drug-related arrests.

If you have suspicions about the potential tenant, or even an established tenant occupying your property, don't hesitate to call the police. Inform the police that you suspect there might be a drug or crime occurring in your property.

The police need definite proof of drug use or drug distribution. But once you report to them, it's on record and they can start observing the various activities going on. As far as I can determine, in most states you have a right to contact the police and/or the sheriff's office with drug-related information.

Deadbeats

The next category of least-desirable tenants is the "All American Deadbeat." Deadbeats are people who don't pay their bills and don't have any intention of paying them unless they are absolutely forced into it. And when they are forced into making a decision about their financial obligations, deadbeats will file bankruptcy rather than pay.

It is my recommendation that you make every attempt to keep those individuals out of your rental unit. People who don't pay their bills as tenants can and will become a financial drain and money problem for you and put you through mountains of frustration and anxiety.

I have 30 years of experience in dealing with people who don't pay their bills. With my experience, I think I can pass on to you sufficient information to help guide you through the process of dealing with this number-one landlord problem concerning finances.

Let me add this note here. If people can prove to you that they were forced into bankruptcy for medical reasons, and I'm sure you know very well that medical expenses can be devastating, I would give some consideration to renting to them if the remainder of their credit record and application to rent is satisfactory.

At any rate, here are some problem solvers to help guide you through processing tenants so you don't end up with a deadbeat.

Solution Number One for Deadbeats

Have I oversold the idea of using a credit bureau? Perhaps. However, I can tell you this. Almost always that deadbeat can be detected and thoroughly screened with a credit report. I will admit that a credit report might not be 100-percent perfect, but it's the best method I've found in screening deadbeats and better than any other method I know.

If you check the credit reports of applicants and find that their records are filled with a list of past-due bills and past-due rent that have been turned over for collection, that's as good a warning as you're going to get. With this information, you can save yourself a lot of trouble. This credit information gives you every right to refuse to rent and will save you some of the following problems.

The Cost of Tenants Who Don't Pay Their Bills

If, on the other hand, you don't care to spend the money for a credit report and you decide not to obtain a credit report or investigate any past rental history, and you "eyeball" the individual, you can expect trouble.

If you become careless and rent your property to people who don't pay their bills, you'll discover that getting rid of them is not easy. Eviction of a deadbeat can be costly. Get them out of your property.

These people just don't pay any bills—their rent or other financial obligations. In addition to not paying their rent, you might be faced with the possibility that they won't pay their utilities. In some cases, those unpaid utilities are charged back to the property owner.

What I find especially revealing in the rental business is that people who don't pay their bills, and frankly don't plan on paying, will fleece anyone and everyone as long as they can. And that includes the landlord.

Whose Fault Is It, Anyway?

In dealing with deadbeats, eventually they will make up stories and present you with all sorts of excuses why they can't pay their bills and have poor credit records. For instance, a common theme these people use is that it's always someone else that caused their financial problems or that "someone" has taken advantage of them, or other similar excuses.

If they've written a bad check, they invariably will insist that it's the bank that made a mistake, not them. And of course the most famous story of all time when it comes time to collect the rent, a story we've all heard many times, and you'll hear it again if the rent is past due, "The check is in the mail."

Slick Methods of Beating the System

The "professional deadbeat" usually is not stupid. Most of them have been beating the system for many years and know just how to work it. To get your confidence, they have the ability to operate very smoothly, talk a good game, and have a unique capacity to take their time obtaining your trust. Eventually you might get to the point where you actually believe their stories, especially if you haven't checked them out.

If you take on a deadbeat tenant, here's what you can expect. And this information I pass on to you is from my experience and other landlords I know in the rental business. The deadbeat will pay the rent for the first two or three months to establish your trust. You begin to believe that you've made the right decision in renting to them. At this point the deadbeat tenant has the hook in.

They prey on you. There'll be times when they get you to the point where you're beginning to feel sorry for them. I honestly know some landlords who are sucked into this situation and believe them. These landlords, and I know some of them, insist "that nice person (the tenant) would never cheat me. Eventually I'm going to get my rent." For some reason or another, some of these landlords just think they have a way about them that no one will cheat on them. Believe me; that's wrong thinking.

The first stage of activities is you'll receive a "honey coated" call, something like this. "Is it OK if I pay the rent on the 15th of the month? I had to pay my car insurance and I just don't have the money right now."

Stage two. They might pay on the 15th, again to gain your trust. The trouble, of course, is that the next monthly rent payment is due in

15 days. That means in 15 days they have to come up with a full month's rent and then in 15 more days the next full month's rent.

Stage three. Eventually deadbeat tenants will call and literally "unload" their woes on you. They've got all sorts of sad stories. They lost their job or they're disabled and can't work.

The next month's rent comes due, and sure enough, they won't have the money. Another call. "Is it alright if I pay you at the end of the month?"

That probably will be the last call, and from then on you are in for a no-win confrontation because they just don't have the money and won't pay the rent. Now they're into you for a full month's past-due rent. At that point the buildup becomes a rolling snowball effect, one month after another.

Stage four. As you pursue efforts to collect past-due rent, pretty soon those tenants will turn on you. They'll get angry with you and blame you for all of their problems. They'll use all sorts of excuses not to pay the rent. They'll say that the apartment was not livable, there was no heat, the stove or refrigerator or washer didn't work And despite the fact that their stories aren't true, they can create such a problem that the entire issue turns into a bloodbath. I've seen it happen.

Stage five. All sorts of hostility sets in, and from that point on you have a major rent-collecting problem. This is a technique the deadbeats have mastered, and believe me; they have no conscience and will use it on anyone and everyone.

Deadbeats Attract More Deadbeats

In addition, you could be faced with the following problem. The "professional deadbeats" are usually lazy and have minimum-wage jobs, if any job at all. And they attract others just like themselves.

I know a landlord who got stuck with a deadbeat. He told me that this unemployed tenant hung around the apartment all day. He attracted visitors who were other lazy, unemployed friends. These so-called friends started hanging out at the deadbeat's apartment. Pretty soon other tenants start complaining about "these people" hanging around the building all day long.

Hence a new problem. The good, reliable, rent-paying tenants threatened to give notice of moving if the landlord didn't do something.

The landlord's problems didn't end there. The deadbeat tenant was not paying the rent, other tenants were complaining, and the deadbeat tenant knew how to act dumb and how to work the system. He had already learned the laws of eviction that protect him. He easily stretched out the longevity and hung on for two more months, even after the landlord proceeded with an eviction notice.

Hence, a costly avoidable lesson. The next step is to do everything possible to get that tenant out of the building so you can establish a new, reliable tenant.

Solution

What can you do if tenants show no indication or willingness that they're going to move? My suggestion is this. The deadbeat, like the drug user, needs and wants money.

That being the case, here's a radical solution that might work. At least it's worth a try. Offer $100 to an in-house tenant you want to get rid of, and offer to forgive any past-due rent if they move out immediately. Try it. If that doesn't work, the next step is collecting past-due rent.

Solution

How do you protect yourself from getting caught in this "dead-beat" mess? Here are some proven methods that can help. First of all, make sure you have every tenant fill out an application for rent. Secondly, analyze that application to the fullest. And then probably the most important method is to obtain a credit report.

Collecting Past-Due Rent from a Deadbeat

Once a deadbeat tenant moves out, the next problem is trying to collect past-due rent. I'll be honest with you and tell you there's little or no solution. You might just as well know right now that it's nearly impossible.

If you pursue past-due rent through the courts, you can bet that the deadbeat will have the same sob story and "honey-soaked" conversation with the judge. From my experience in the court system, that deadbeat is going to tell the judge that it's all your fault and that you did not provide proper and livable accommodations. And the judge will eat all this up. I have found that most judges have a prejudice and aren't interested in protecting any rich landlord.

Renting to a deadbeat does nothing to increase your net worth and income. And renting to a deadbeat creates more problems and anxiety than you want to deal with. It's flawed thinking if you believe you can rent to a deadbeat tenant. You simply don't need him.

I recommend that you use the credit bureau to collect any and all past-due rent. I don't believe it's a good idea to waste your valuable time trying to collect those bills. Use that time to manage the good tenants and take care of your property.

Let the credit bureau deal with collections. They have the experience and know how. Undoubtedly that bureau will have other collections against this individual or individuals and will just include yours right along with the others.

And let me add one more significant fact. Don't expect the credit bureau to get your money overnight. Don't call at the end of the month and ask the credit bureau if they've collected your rent. It takes time dealing with these kinds of people. When they collect the money, they'll pay you.

Transient Laborers

Transient, construction, day laborers come and go. Most are short-term renters. I've contacted real estate investors who have rented to transient laborers, and here's what they told me.

You can count on the fact that there's going to be damage to the property. Transient laborers, for the most part, are smokers. Part of the cleanup will be getting rid of the smoke smell through out the entire unit. Smokers also burn holes in the carpet, the bedding, along kitchen counters, in and around the bathroom vanity and sink, and most any other place in the unit.

Not only are transient laborers smokers, but they are also drinkers. The combination isn't a pleasant prospect. When it comes time to call attention to some problem within the rental unit, when confronted, drinkers often become belligerent, and it's not unusual to find holes in the walls from such quarrelsome behavior.

One major problem in renting to transient laborers, something that can be alarming to most landlords, is the fact that once that transient laborer makes a commitment to rent the unit, you never know who all and how many are going to show up and move in. It can be 1, and it can end up being 10 people living in the same apartment and using the facilities. It happens.

Leaving in the Middle of the Night

When the construction project is completed, they sometimes leave in the middle of the night without giving any notification. As I've visited with some of my landlord friends, they tell me that some of these people will leave and give no forwarding address. If the rent is past due when the work-job is completed and they're gone, you will have a difficult time collecting.

Next comes the additional cost of cleaning up the mess after they leave. There's garbage and junk and beer bottles and filled ashtrays. They tend to leave used, worn-out work shoes; old, dirty clothing; mattresses, beds, davenports, and even old TVs. It's all worthless garbage and junk, and you pay for the cleanup.

Here's an interesting story about just such an occurrence where this tenant moved out without giving notice, with rent past due, and with a pile of junk left in the apartment and yard. My friend, the landlord, discovered that the tenant didn't move out of the community, but just across town. The tenant left trash in the yard and in the apartment that included some old tires, beer bottles, an old davenport, and bags of garbage. My friend loaded all of this junk on his pickup, took it over to the new address, and dumped it all in the front yard. The tenant confronted him and wanted to know what he was doing. My friend, with a smile on his face, responded by saying, "You forgot some of your property and I'm just delivering it to you." And away he went. My friend didn't make any money doing this, but at least it gave him the satisfaction of getting even.

Animal-Care People

I've said that a lot of people in the health field make good tenants. However, there is this exception—animal-care people. And here's the reason why.

Some animal-care people will bring in sick animals overnight to watch them. These ill animals will lie around and vomit or urinate on the carpet. It's nearly impossible to get rid of the smell, especially cat urine. This means you could end up tearing out and replacing good carpeting.

Most of the people in the animal-care business wear boots. As they go trudging through the animal barns, pigpens, into and through yards just plain filled with animal waste products, those boots become infiltrated with manure and barnyard waste. They return to their apartments with little concern about cleaning up, and you can be sure that the smell follows them right into their living quarters.

I have a friend who said that the smell got so bad that the carpet had to be removed and that the actual floorboards had to be torn out. The smell had penetrated into the wood, and it was impossible to get rid of it.

Student Housing

Let me preface this by saying that there are and can be some good student tenants. So, whatever you do, don't overlook them. Seek out the good ones.

However, deciding which students make good tenants is part of the landlording business. How does one go about screening and finding them? With students this can be a major problem for almost all landlords.

Most students, and especially freshmen, have little if any credit history or even a credit file. Most of them are only 18, 19, or 20 years old. With freshmen, there usually aren't any landlord references because the students have just left their "mothers' cocoons" and their family homes.

Freshmen can and do create problems. They've just been released from the "high school" protective and suppressive environment. Now they're out on their own, and they feel it's time to let loose. They are no longer subjected to various degrees of suppression, both in high school and at home, so they're free to do just as they please.

Here's another fact about college freshman. Out of 100 freshmen that enter college, only 33 eventually continue their education and graduate with a degree.

Coming from a college community, I can tell you that these factors indicate that some of those 67 percent are there the first year to raise hell. And what all this means is parties, girls, beer, and wild times.

There are serious problems to consider when renting to students. Here are some of them:

- Loud music
- Parties
- Liquor
- Highly testosterone-charged boys either renting or visiting the premises

If you own a multiunit apartment building and one apartment of students plays loud music day and night, you know you've got a problem with the other tenants. Possibly an exception to this is if the entire apartment complex is rented to students. Then you can let them control the noise and parties.

I have a friend who owned an off-campus apartment. He said that there were constant complaints from neighbors and from the police regarding late-night, boisterous beer parties. In the spring of the year, when testosterone is flowing at its peak, it was not unusual that the police would call and tell the landlord that there were 30 or 40 students, along with beer kegs, partying all night inside and in the front yard. Most of the time the police would make a call and tell the participant to quiet down, but rarely did they do anything further. So the question is, what can a landlord do if the police can't handle it?

My friend told me that he put up with this for a couple of years. He said it was a good money maker, but there was just too much trouble to deal with, and it was not worth it. He sold the property and got out of the student rental business.

If a student is not self-supporting, you have every right to reject her on the basis of insufficient income, no credit, and no rental experience. If students don't have rental experience or credit, and you still think you want to rent to them, one method of assuring yourself of getting the rent money is to have the parents sign the lease, that is if they have a good record.

Some junior and senior students can and do make satisfactory tenants. They've matured and grown and have become more serious about their education.

Another factor when renting to students is that a college school year ends in 9 months, not 12. Even though you might have the student sign a 12-month lease, it's not easy to enforce this addendum. It's almost impossible to get students to fulfill a 12-month lease if after 9 months they're leaving town. They might sign the lease, but making them fulfill it is something else.

Here's another problem that can and does occur with some students. Let's say you've rented an apartment to two female students. A boyfriend comes to visit his girlfriend. He, of course, makes himself at home. He takes off his shoes, he might or might not have smelly feet, drinks beer, and upsets the calm and quiet of the living space. Eventually the nonmated roommate gets irritated living in these conditions. She decides she's had enough and moves out. This creates all sorts of landlord problems. Who pays the rent? Who's responsible for the rent deposit, and who pays the utilities?

Solution

With these problems in mind, here are some helpful suggestions when renting to student tenants:

1. Rent the unit restricting occupancy to two students only per apartment.

   (Establish a strict policy of renting only to two students per apartment and make sure more don't move in after the lease is signed. The

more students, the more wear and tear and heavy use of the rental unit and facilities.)

2. Make sure to confirm that those who sign the lease know that each is responsible.

   (In my experience, one of the tricks some students try to pull is leaving without notification with rent due. When you contact the students, they'll always say it's the other person who didn't pay. Don't rent to students without letting them know that they are all responsible for the rent. That way they can't blame each other for past-due rent, especially blaming the other person who's already moved out and gone.)

3. Often students will leave at the end of the school year, which rarely coincides with the rental agreement and is often in the middle of the month before the lease is up.

   (Usually what can happen is there isn't enough rent deposit to cover all the expenses in addition to an extra month's rent.)

4. Demand sufficient rent deposit money to make up for any losses and try to set up a rent deposit for damage, and a rent deposit for the last month's rent.

5. Let students know they cannot leave an accumulation of "junk."

   (When there are several students in the unit, they tend to live in slovenly conditions. None of them wants to accept the responsibility for anything, especially cleaning up after they leave.

   When they moved in, most of this "junk" could have been handed down from one student to another or thrown away by someone else. Some of it is old, run-down furniture they received from their parents. Most of it was free, so it's easy just to ignore it and leave it.

   In my experience most of the junk they leave includes old davenports and chairs, old mattresses and beds, and various items of furniture too numerous to mention, all of which are old and worn out, with no value whatsoever.

   Here's one specific experience I had. I rented an apartment to four student athletes, primarily football players. This turned out to be a

mistake and bad move on my part. I should have known better. There's a name for this kind of carelessness. It's called stupid. *Anyway, when they moved out, they left a mess. It took a great deal of work and time to clean up their eyesore.*

They left a set of barbells; some old, worn-out exercise equipment; old tennis shoes; athletic equipment; and one set of golf clubs. Fortunately, I had a large storage space in the basement where I put all of this junk because I didn't want to take chances on their coming back and claiming I threw away their "highly valuable" personal property. If I had thrown that junk away, it would have suddenly, in their minds, become valuable. At any rate, they didn't come back, and after six months or so I had to have it hauled away, and you know who paid.)

6. Students often leave at the end of the school year in the middle of the month. The time often depends on tests. Usually they don't notify you and this means there's no proper 30-day notice given. That's why landlords need a rent deposit. Students won't be around to pay the next month's rent.

Solution

Once that tenant is gone, you certainly don't want to show a new potential tenant an abandoned unit. This means it's got to be cleaned up and the carpet must be cleaned. It also might call for painting. To prepare the unit and get it ready for the next tenant takes time, money, and in all likelihood the loss of a month's rent.

And I can assure you that all students don't go to Panama City, Florida, for spring break. Some stay on campus or in apartments. And believe me, when there's a combination of boys with high levels of testosterone, girls, and beer, this equals noisy, wild, and disorderly parties. In the cold-weather states, this occurs during the spring of the year and at the end of school the year. It's hard to control, but if you have an awareness of this, you might want to have something written in your lease so you can protect yourself.

Cover yourself through your rent or lease contract with sufficient rent deposit for the removal of sofas, mattresses, or whatever items are left. You can always refund that part of the deposit once the unit is cleaned up and inspected. Also have sufficient rent deposit to cover any past-due rent.

Relatives and Friends and Relatives' Friends

If you want to know what real trouble is in the rental business, rent to an irresponsible relative, friend, or a friend of a relative. When you start negotiating with these people, you'll find that the friend or relative will be *very* friendly. They will make all sorts of promises to you about what good tenants they're going to be, and that they'll help look after your property.

What you don't know is that once they're settled in, they will be demanding and become constant complainers. Most of the time they'll use those complaints for excuses about why they don't pay their rent. When they complain they'll expect you to jump through hoops to fix this or fix that whenever they call.

But most importantly, once they get behind on rent they assume, because of your friendship or relationship, it's OK and you won't bother them. After all, you're a friend or relative and they expect you to understand that as a friend or relative you won't press them for payment. They assume you're a "rich landlord."

Once they get to the point of being several months behind on rent, and if you put the pressure on them for payment or threaten them with eviction, it places you in a nearly impossible situation. At this point, friend or relative, they'll start taking it out on you. They become angry at you and blame you for everything, even their own personal problems. And there's a good chance you could get sucked into their personal problems, family, money, health, sympathy, or just about anything.

Everything then really turns from bad to worse. Here's what you can expect. In all probability, your relationships will deteriorate from friends or relatives to arch enemies. You'll also be out several months' rental income.

If your "friendly" tenants, or any tenants for that matter, get really angry at you, there's a possibility that they might even destroy your property before they leave. You can also count on their leaving, usually in the dead of night, with no intention of giving any notification. For sure they aren't about to clean up the unit or pay any past-due rent.

Previous Landlord Negative History

If you know that the applicant had a negative report from a previous landlord, don't think that you can rent to that person and she will have changed her ways. She won't.

Be careful that you don't get caught in a "discrimination" trap. Therefore, keep records of interviews pertaining to the rejection. Specifically state in the record the reason for the decline, such as loud parties, poor history of paying rent, drugs, or any other negative information, and the time and date.

Inadequate Credit Information

If the applicant doesn't have any credit information, you have a right to refuse to rent. If this should occur, notify that person the specific reason for the decline.

Insufficient Income to Pay Rent

Of course, it's important for you to know that the tenant has sufficient income to pay the rent. How best to do this? Call the employer and ask for the personnel office. Verify the applicant's job status, length of time working there, and income. A second method of verifying income is to ask applicants for some proof of their monthly income. This can be a copy of a paycheck.

Another consideration is this. Maybe that person has sufficient income. However, after you've done the credit bureau check and you find that the applicant owes a lot of unpaid obligations, ask the applicant or ask yourself, will the applicant have enough income to pay a car payment and/or other bills with sufficient income to pay the rent?

I make it a policy to let the tenants know that rent comes first in paying their obligations. If you find that there isn't sufficient income to pay the rent and you decline the individual, keep a good record of your conversation, including dates and times and the specific reason for refusal.

Con Artists

If you have an individual coming to rent an apartment and he tells you that he played football with the Green Bay Packers, beware. That statement is made with tongue in cheek, but it's to illustrate how con artists work.

Solution

Avoid these problem tenants before you're caught in a financial loss. Problem tenants can cause anxiety and heart attacks.

Chapter 4

Discrimination
Laws

It's wonderful to operate a business without the stress and strain of having to worry or be concerned about a lawsuit. One of the most important facts that I can pass on to you regarding discrimination lawsuits is this: Be thoroughly informed regarding your specific state discrimination laws. They can and do vary from state to state.

The Fair Housing Law, dated 1968, with amendments, covers fair housing and discrimination laws throughout the United States. The federal agency that controls fair housing is the U.S. Department of Housing and Urban Development by the Assistant Secretary for Fair Housing and Equal Opportunity, Washington D.C., 20410. Phone 1-800-669-9777. I hope you never have to call them. Therefore, I recommend this: Do everything in your power to protect your investment business from discrimination lawsuits.

Federal Discrimination Laws

Basically, here is what the discrimination law regarding rental property says:

> *Everyone, regardless of sex, race, color, religion, ancestry or national origin are free and equal and are entitled to full and equal accommodations and facilities.*

I think it's important to expand that list, so here's a cautionary catalogue of some of the very basic and hard-core issues that should raise a red flag for every landlord. These are the kinds of issues that attorneys target.

- Age
- Race
- Color
- Religion
- Sex
- Same-sex marriage
- Marital status
- Sexual orientation
- Gays
- Lesbians
- Unmarried couples
- Familial status
- Handicap
- National origin
- Receipt of public assistance
- Political party membership
- Unregistered foreigners
- Family size
- Student status

Solution

Don't Create Problems if There Aren't Any

Don't let your prejudices rule your business life. More simply put, use common sense. If some of or any of the above-mentioned issues and lifestyles bother you—unmarried couples living together, homosexual marriages, lesbians and gays living together—it might be a signal that you should consider investing in some business other than the rental business.

Here is one area where the landlord is somewhat protected. If you have rental property for senior citizens only, you can discriminate on the basis of age. What that means is if an applicant with children applies, you can reject the application.

Solution

Protect Your Investment

The second and equally important piece of information I want to pass on is this. Contact your insurance agent and have the agent review your entire insurance program. Above all, and this is something we overlook, make sure you have adequate coverage in the event that you should ever be sued under the Fair Housing Act.

Avoid Sexual Harassment

As a landlord you should know that the U.S. Department of Housing and Urban Development has taken a strong stand against sexual harassment. Sexual harassment laws are explicitly covered in the Fair

Housing Act. You as a landlord should be made aware of these laws and what they can do to you and your business.

The single biggest concern of every landlord, and the one that I think is more prevalent with the most ramifications, is asking a tenant to exchange sex for rent. Even if you, as a landlord, make any intimate conversation with the tenant or inquire about the tenant's love life, you're asking for trouble.

You can also be vulnerable if you're confronted with an irate tenant that owes you rent who wants to get back at you. Even though nothing sexually occurred, a tenant can file a false claim for sexual harassment for some minor incident or comment you might have made. It can and has happened.

If and when it should be a case of the tenant filing a complaint, it becomes a point of the tenant's word against the landlord's word. It's often a tough case to prove. But there are no winners. You might not lose the court case, if it gets to that point, but it's time-consuming, financially consuming, and emotionally consuming. You can imagine that, even if there is no proof of sexual harassment, it's nearly impossible to clear your name with your friends, your family, or just about anyone.

Solution

Don't Take Chances

Don't even think of taking chances. If and when you observe a nice-looking person, and the thought goes through your mind that you think you might make some sort of offer to a tenant, it's time to get out of there and get home as quickly as possible. When you get home, take a cold shower or whatever it takes, but don't fool around and become involved with your tenant.

Do you know what they call people who get themselves into this kind of situation? *Stupid*. Then I thought, do you suppose someone is sitting in an office or living room and reading this and saying, "That guy is stupid; he doesn't know what he's been missing." Of course my second reaction is, it's not worth it.

Teenager Wins Big Settlement

Here's how one landlord was able to decrease his net worth and lose his reputation, possibly some of his real estate, and probably his insurance coverage. This particular case occurred in New York. The landlord and owner of an apartment building confronted his 19-year-old tenant and offered her free rent in exchange for sexual favors. She, of course, refused and hired an attorney. The attorney sued the landlord. That landlord, and I'm assuming the insurance company, paid something like $400,000 + in a settlement.

Bold but Not Too Bright

Here's an actual newspaper ad dated 8-25-02:

> *For Rent: 2 Bedroom, heat paid, $725. Must have sex with landlord.*

It's not necessary to say much more.

Another Case of Not Being Too Bright

This tenant made application for rent. When she completed the application, the landlord asked her, "Does your boyfriend come to visit and jump your bones?" This tenant went to Legal Aid Services, a free service for limited-income people, and they filed a lawsuit.

Apparently, it was learned in the lawsuit that this was his way of presenting to her the opportunity to give sex if she ever got behind on her rent. He denied that anything like that occurred. However, he didn't come right out and say it, but from the question it was the inference and innuendo.

He, or his insurance company, paid $12,500, which included attorney fees and a civil penalty. Interestingly, here's what the landlord said after the case was settled. "She owed me $1200 in rent. I imagine she figured this lawsuit, which was unfounded, was a way to get back at me. I guess she did."

Mississippi Sex Case

The Justice Department, working with the Housing and Urban Development Department, filed a case against a landlord who demanded sex for rent from various female tenants. This operation had apparently been going on for some time. What really got the landlord in major trouble was the fact that if the tenant refused to provide sex, he evicted her. Judgment was issued against the landlord in the amount of $451,000. Do you think that landlord was missing some important brain cells?

Landlord Wins Discrimination Case Against Attorney

The following case is taken from a book titled *LANDLORDING*, written by Leigh Robinson, published by Express, PO Box 1639, El Cerrito, CA., with his permission.

I quote the article in Chapter 11, Page 206.

In New York, there was a case regarding a landlord who refused to rent to someone for one reason only, because that person was an attorney. The attorney-applicant sued, arguing that wholesale discrimination against attorneys was illegal. The landlord responded that attorneys eat landlords for breakfast, that as a whole they are more argumentative and more likely to sue than other people; hence they are more likely to make bad tenants. Amazingly enough, the court sided with the landlord in the case, and that decision made national news. (Perhaps the case merely showed that attorneys are even less sympathetic figures than landlords.)

Government Attorneys

Unfortunately, there are not only private legal professionals who find every excuse to start legal action, but also there are government-paid advocates who are sitting on the sideline like a flock of vultures waiting for some excuse to start legal action—especially against landlords.

We, as real estate investors, find it necessary to keep a watchful eye for government-subsidized, bureaucratic legal aid services. Most of those hired are waiting for any excuse to file lawsuits to fill their workload. They know how vulnerable landlords can be and that they can get settlements and judgments and awards against those "rich landlords."

One could easily say, "Yeah, there's always a judge that will make an accurate decision." Do you think so? Judges are advanced people in the legal profession. Do you think they have justice and fairness in mind when dealing with "rich landlord versus the poor tenant? Sometimes I wonder.

Federal Government Advocacy Groups

Legal Aid Services is a "government agency legal system," a legal system totally financed by the federal government. Salaries, rents, and all expenses are paid by the government. And I don't have to remind you where the government gets its money.

Individuals practicing in these offices are paid a basic salary. They don't rely on how much they earn or how many cases they win. They are paid win or lose and keep their job on the basis of having a full "work" load of cases. The more cases they accumulate, the more they can *brag* about their overload of work to their bureaucratic supervisors. That's the way the system works. That's how they stay on the government payroll, sucking up to their superiors. It appears that they do a pretty good job of this, sucking up, because rarely do you hear of any government attorney being fired.

What does all this mean? It means this for the real estate investor. In all probability, whoever walks into the legal-aid office becomes a case. And believe me, they will stretch the imagination of that case to make sure they look intelligent and busy and keep an open workload.

This I can tell you. These attorneys prey on hospitals, landlords, Credit Bureaus, and collection agencies. Who qualifies to use these services? It is said that this is legal representation for low-income people. I don't know what criteria they use to determine who is low income, but there are lots of them.

Some probably view legal aid as part of "creeping socialism." As far as I know there are legal aid offices all over the country, in every state, and sometimes in every county.

Interestingly, and it's important for you to know, they always have the upper hand. They are relentless in pursuing their cases. The reason for this, right or wrong, is it makes them look good and it increases their workload and justifies their existence. Those people must keep busy in order to keep their government-paid jobs.

The Legal System Baiting Landlords

There are baiters set up in these offices calling themselves testers. The testers, who can be just about anyone working in any number of these government offices, are checking on landlords to see if they can trap them into refusing to rent, show, or even talk to certain potential tenants. It's kind of like the *60 Minutes* TV show; they're out to catch you doing something illegal.

A landlord's fact of life is that lawyers like to bait landlords. They place an office in a community and start calling want ads. They represent themselves as potential tenants and as minorities and bait you the landlord. If, after the interview, you refuse to rent to them, you're in for a stack of discrimination trouble. Don't trust them. It's a fact of landlord life.

In our community, Legal Aid staff members would get someone in their office, usually someone with an ethnic background, to call answering an ad for rental property. They'd call landlords and represent themselves as other than what they were, not really wanting to rent the unit but trying to lead landlords into committing a discrimination. This happens especially in an ethnically mixed community.

This list of questions was drawn up and prepared by the Fair Housing Council. Whoever called would have the list right there in front of them and start the conversation. Having inside legal advice, you know that they were most likely well prepared for the interview. In that preparation they were probably told to be assertive and get right in with their questions.

- Is the place still available?
- Can I move in immediately?
- Are all the facts and rent amount correct as stated?
- Are there any special rules?
- Are pets allowed?
- Do I have to fill out a rent application form?
- Do I need references?

Here's what they look for once the questions are answered and the call is completed:

"Answers to the questions over the phone will provide a check on whether landlords give you the same information when you see them in person. If your race or nationality can be identified by your voice, have someone else make the call for you. If you are given different information in person than you received over the phone, you may be a victim of discrimination. If you suspect discrimination, report the situation to Fair Housing Services."

They make sure see that all the answers you give are the same for each caller inquiring about the unit. Different answers means they consider this as reason to believe there's discrimination.

Solution

Use Common Sense

Here's what I've done. When I get a call and I'm asked a question, before I respond, I say, "Wait a minute. Who is this calling? I can't tell you anything until you tell me who's calling." If they don't respond, I don't want to talk to them. Then if we get to the point where they've identified themselves and they want to ask questions, here's how I would respond:

- When asked if the place is still available, the answer is, "Yes, but I'm taking calls, and when I get all the calls in, I will make a decision and get back to you."
- Can I move in immediately? The same answer applies.
- As far as rent amount is concerned, there should be no reason to change this.
- If you have a no-pet policy, stick with it no matter what.
- Do I have to fill out a rent application form? The answer is yes, and that yes is to everyone.
- And the rent application form specifically asks for references.

Their system of baiting worked for a while, but pretty soon everyone in the rental business caught on to it. From what I recall, I read someplace that the legal aid people got themselves in trouble doing this. So as far as I know, I don't think they do it anymore. However, wherever there's a potential lawsuit, there might be other private and not government attorneys out there that might attempt to trap you.

If you get the feeling every once in a while when you're reading this that I'm chicken when it comes to anything to do with the legal business, you're right. I am chicken. I've never been sued and don't want to be. But I know of people who have been sued, that weren't even at fault, and it cost them a fortune to clear their names. The point is, beware.

Chapter 5

Avoiding Rejection Lawsuits

L isten. If you want to protect yourself from getting involved in a disagreeable tenant-lawyer dispute or confrontation that could lead to a lawsuit, it's going to take some preliminary work, time, and effort on your part to establish that protection.

Nobody ever said the landlording business was easy; it can be enjoyable and profitable, but at times might not be all that easy.

Do Not Reject for Any of the Following Reasons

To establish discrimination and rejection protection, let's take a look at some of the following troublesome areas. I'd suggest that you "red flag" any of these as a potential lawsuit. If you reject or discriminate against a tenant for any of the following reasons, you're breaking the law and subjecting yourself to litigation. Here they are again:

- Race
- Color
- Religion
- Ethic background
- National origin
- Sexual orientation
- Marital status
- Disability
- Reliance on public assistance
- People with children

The Landlord's Right of Rejection and Refusal

Despite the fact that the landlord is subjected to many discrimination laws, there are laws that give rights to protect landlords and their property. And you, as a landlord, have a right to reject an applicant for many reasons. I'm calling your attention to some of the most obvious reasons that can be used for refusal or rejection.

The Right of Refusal: Drugs and Crime

If the applicant or applicants have had any dealings whatsoever with using, selling, purchasing, manufacturing, or distributing illegal drugs, you have a right of refusal to rent. If any applicant has possession of illegal firearms or stolen property, you have a right to refuse to rent. If you find an applicant who has been involved with promoting, selling, or representing prostitution, you have a right to refuse rental. This might be rare, but it is possible.

The Right of Refusal: The Credit Report

The most common and most frequently applied reason for rejection is the credit report. As a landlord, you must protect yourself with every means available. Don't even think about renting to anyone without obtaining a credit report.

All the information about the benefits of the credit report are covered in a separate chapter in its entirety. However, let's review some of that important credit information that's worth telling you about to support your right to refusal or rejection.

For instance, there's sufficient information in a credit report that can give you plenty of data about the character and pay record of the individual. This factual information presents to you a solid method of rejecting a potential tenant.

If applicants for your rental unit don't pay their bills; if they have suits and judgments, liens, or bankruptcies; if they have records of past-due rent that has been turned over for collection; or if they don't have sufficient income to pay the rent; you have every legal right to turn them down.

Responsibilities of a Credit Rejection

If you decline any individual on the basis of the information you received from the Credit Bureau, here are some basic steps to take to protect yourself.

- You must give that individual a copy of the credit file.
     (You paid for it, so be sure the credit agency gives you a copy of the report, and keep it in your file.)
- Notify the individual that it was not the Credit Bureau that turned them down as a tenant.
- Tell them the refusal was based on the information acquired from the Credit Bureau.
- If that person disputes the information on the credit report, cease all communication at this point and tell the individual or individuals, "I have to decline your application for rental on the basis of the

information I received from the Credit Bureau. I have no control over the information I've received in the report."

The Do's and Don'ts

Once you've confronted the individuals or individual and advised them that you do not care to have them as tenants, the next step is to be cautious in dealing with them. My advice is to take the following steps:

- Don't become personally involved with their problems.

    (You're going to be confronted by that individual or individuals, and they're going to dispute the information. They'll tell you, "That's not my collection," or "Those bills are all paid in full.")

- Don't get involved and try to analyze the credit report. That's not your business.

    (That's the obligation and responsibility of the credit reporting agency.)

- Don't get involved with any lengthy discussion about the credit report.

    (If you do, you're going into a losing battle and you won't win.)

- Don't get into any argument or feud.
- Don't personally consider it as your decision or fault.

    (Your decision is simply to tell the applicants they do not qualify as tenants under your regulations.)

- Do tell the applicants, "These are not my records, and it's very important that you contact the credit reporting agency."
- Do give them directions for finding the Credit Bureau. Inform them that they have a right to contact that agency and confront them if there's any information that is disputed in their file.
- Do tell the individual or individuals that from that point it's out of your hands and, again, this is entirely up to that credit agency to work out any controversial ratings or disputes.
- Do make every attempt to cover yourself.

    (It might be a good idea to end the conversation by saying, "Once you clear up your credit report, you can come back and reapply.")

- Do keep written records of your conversation with the potential tenant with all the details.

The Right of Refusal: Previous Landlord's Negative Recommendaton

In addition to acquiring the all-important credit report, don't hesitate to contact the previous landlords. If in your research and investigation you learn from the previous landlord or landlords that the applicant was an undesirable tenant, caused physical damage to the property, caused complaints of loud music and loud parties from other tenants, didn't pay the rent on time, or were dealing in drugs, there's one quick way to handle the situation.

Emphatically inform them, "From what I've learned from your previous landlord and on the basis of your past experience as a renter, I'm not interested in having you as a tenant."

In all likelihood, you might find that individual or those individuals will dispute what was said about them. Avoid any such confrontation. Simply tell them, "You'll have to contact your previous landlord, and you should be able to find the details and work out any disputes you have."

The previous landlord would probably appreciate this. My guess is that there's a good chance that the tenants owe past-due rent. That means they will have no desire to make contact and be confronted by the previous landlord. But at least you've covered yourself.

The Right to Reject: Damage to Property

If you learn from the previous landlord that the applicants misused the property, this is certainly a right to reject. Once you learn of any problems, confront the applicants and ask them if there was any misunderstanding with their former landlord.

The Right to Reject: Too Many Occupants

Another key factor to protect your property is turning down potential tenants because there are too many occupants. In your interview, ask the applicant how many people will be occupying the rental unit.

If you were informed and they signed a lease that only one or two persons would be living in your rental unit, and you discover, after they've moved in, that there are several people living there, inform them that this is not acceptable. Simply tell them, "The apartment is not large enough to handle more than two people and you were not truthful when you signed your rent application stating there would only be two. Therefore you're either going to move out or have others move out."

You can expect an argument. Their comeback will be, "We think we can all live there, and it is our decision." Answer by telling them, "No, that is my decision." Leave it up to them, but check back and make sure they've made a decision either to move out or have their friends or relatives move out.

When I refuse tenants, on any basis, I tell them why and give them sufficient and well-established facts. And once again, keep good records of the conversation, any confrontation, and the words that were exchanged regarding the entire procedure.

The Right of Refusal: Pets

You have every right to establish a no-pet addendum in your lease. You also have a right of refusal if you have an established no-pet policy, no matter how convincing the tenant might be. You will hear stories about how their pet is harmless, doesn't bark, doesn't urinate on the carpet, and doesn't smell. They do.

In addition, in all my dealings with pets, dog owners *swear* that their dogs never bite. They do. I've also experienced neighbors calling and complaining about dogs barking and running unchained. The dog is penned in all day, and when the owner leaves, the dog or dogs start barking. The owner, of course, is gone and can't hear the barking. There are now dog owners who think one isn't enough; they need two dogs.

Sometimes the problem is this: They say they don't have a pet and don't mention anything about a pet. They move in, and guess what? A pet shows up. Then you're faced with a new problem of what to do.

The only way to solve the problem is to confront them. Remind them that they signed a lease that says no pets. Tell them personally or send them notice that either the pets go from the premises or they go.

The Right of Refusal: Disruptive Activities

If you're real estate investment is located in a college town, you'll learn quickly about loud parties along with loud music. If it's a multiple unit, there's no doubt that these activities will disturb and upset other tenants. If you know this can happen, you can refuse to rent. On the other hand, if they're already in and start these activities, you must take a stand and stop these parties. Again, it is confrontational.

The Right of Refusal: Health Factors

For various health reasons, you have a right to discriminate. Especially refuse to rent to anyone who drinks heavily, and many landlords refuse on the basis of potential tenants who smoke.

The Right of Refusal: False Application

If there's a record of crime that's not reported or any other false information on the rental application, this is grounds for refusal to rent. Often some of that information can and will show up on a credit bureau report.

The Right to Reject: Your Personal Home

Here's a question I've been asked, "If I own a duplex and live in one half, do I have a right to discriminate and chose whomever I wish to occupy the other unit?" Yes, but be careful.

The Importance of Keeping Records

Maintaining good records can avoid future complications. When you've turned down tenants, keep the applications on file for a good period of time. Write the full details and reason for refusal. Include the date and time you contacted the individuals. Keep a record of the conversations. Make certain you record the reason you refused to accept the applicants as tenants.

Why do I insistent on keeping these thorough records? There's always a possibility that you can end up in court defending yourself. One thing I've learned in the court system is if you have well-kept records of dates and conversations, you are in a good position for winning.

I've participated in the court system using the small claims court, also known as conciliation court. Most of the people (tenants) I've observed were rarely prepared to go before a judge. They usually don't have any records whatsoever, and as they enter the courtroom before the judge, they more or less have to blunder through the hearing by not knowing or remembering the specific details of the case. Court judges like good records and accurate information.

Always Make a Thorough Search

Don't take chances when it comes to renting out your personally owned property. After you've done your preliminary investigation, including the rental application and the credit report, if you have some reservations and insecure feelings about that person you're dealing with as a potential tenant, don't hesitate to continue the investigation.

Checking with previous landlords can reveal a great deal of information. You'll be able to find out what kind of a tenant the applicant was, whether she was involved in any controversial activities, including drugs, and whether she was prompt in paying her rent.

For additional information, although it does take some time, contact the office of the Clerk of Court in your county. There are sufficient legal records and documents in the Clerk's office that can help in your decision-making progress. The Clerk of Court records includes suits, judgments, bankruptcies, and criminal records. The data is basically free, or at most provided for a nominal fee.

If you should find any of these items on the individual or individuals in your investigation, that should be enough to tell you to be cautious to say the least. I know I'd be totally discouraged about signing a rental lease. One more source, in smaller cities and communities don't hesitate to check the police records. All of these items, confirmed, with on hand records, gives you sufficient legal justification to reject.

Visiting on Site

Incidentally, a friend of mine in the rental business told me about part of the process he uses to scrutinize his potential tenants and how he completed his investigation. Here, in his words, is what he said.

"When the person calls answering my ad or inquiring about renting, once I conduct a phone interview I can usually tell if I want to pursue this particular person or persons. After a satisfactory credit check, I tell him I'd like to meet him at his current address. I make an appointment and take the time to see his apartment. Once I get there, his lifestyle and housekeeping become apparent to me. From what I observe I can pretty much tell whether I want him to occupy my apartment and whether or not he fits into my desirable or undesirable category. I also know then and there whether or not I want to continue my investigation."

"If I'm satisfied, I make an appointment and have him go to my rental unit."

"If I'm not satisfied, and I've observed that his lifestyle does not fit what I'm looking for as a desirable tenant, I tell him that there have been others who have called about renting and that I have to make contact with them before I make a decision."

"I might say something like, 'I'll get back to you as soon as I've made a decision.'"

As Rejection or Refusal Occur, Close the Case

Whatever you do, don't get into arguments with applicants. Don't participate in name-calling. Just close the case.

Chapter 6

The Legal
System

(Disclaimer)

This Is Simply a Guide Book

This chapter explains how real estate investors can avoid lawsuits, lawyers, and the legal system. This book is not providing legal advice. That being said, before I prepared the information contained in this document, I consulted with my attorney. His advice was to begin by establishing this disclaimer.

He informed me to be specific and make it quite clear to the reader that the publisher, McGraw-Hill, and the author, myself, do not intend to contribute any sort of legal advice to anyone. He further suggested that I make it very clear that I am not practicing law without a license, and neither is the publisher. He said I should not give anyone incorrect advice, inaccurate information, or not enough information regarding the various landlording laws that we'll review. If any information in this document is erroneous, is not intentional. My attorney said, "I suggest that you tell your readers that if they are in need of legal advice of any kind that they consult with an attorney."

He did say this, "Don't scare anyone away from investing in real estate because of the threat of lawsuits or any legal action. Lawsuits usually occur with those who are careless or negligent or who are involved in illegal or criminal activity." If real estate investors operate their businesses according to the laws, there should be no reason to have any apprehension about being in the rental business.

Concern about Legal Action

I personally do have a concern and some apprehension about becoming involved in any sort of legal action, whether it be giving legal advice or suggesting that the legal system can be manipulated in any way whatsoever.

Here's why. Legal issues and litigation can be detrimental and devastating to one's financial position, business operation, and above all, the peace of mind of anyone involved in a lawsuit.

Therefore, the purpose of this section regarding legal issues for landlords is basically to pass on knowledge from my own real estate experiences and the experiences of others whom I've interviewed.

It is my hope that the knowledge can be used as a guide and help you protect your business from becoming engaged in any potential legal issues or litigation. To be totally honest with you, there simply are too many laws regarding landlording. That alone makes it virtually impossible to cover them all. And more importantly, it's impossible to give precise advice about understanding each of these laws governing the landlording and real estate investment business. It is therefore my recommendation that if you have any serious legal questions or issues regarding your real estate business, seek professional legal services to ensure that you are operating within the legal system.

Everyone Needs an Attorney

I personally believe that it's best to establish you and your business with one reliable attorney and stick with whomever you choose. It would also be my recommendation that you establish yourself with an attorney whom you can consider a personal friend. That shouldn't be difficult because most of the attorneys I know are amiable and personable.

I can truthfully say that my attorney is honest, trustworthy, and reliable. I can count on him to look after and protect my interests. It is only a minority of attorneys involved in the judiciary system who upset some of our lives. Obviously not everyone involved in the legal profession should be branded a pettifogger.

But it's important to realize that in the real world of real estate investment, there are legal vulnerability issues, and legal participants who look for and seek out these problems. These are matters that should be of concern to every investor.

Everyone in the real estate investment business needs, at various times, legal services and guidance. For instance, if you're about to purchase real estate you definitely need an attorney to examine the abstract to make sure you are getting a clear title to the property. Few of us can do this on our own. This is something you certainly don't want to overlook.

You need an attorney to protect your investment and be assured that there aren't unpaid bills, judgments, or encumbrances against that property. You also want an attorney to examine the deed transferring the property into your name to make sure it's correct. This work, done by an attorney, is inexpensive insurance.

Here's a specific case where the legal advice from my attorney kept me from getting involved in a situation that could have been costly and time-consuming. I had been contacted by a realtor regarding a single-family home. It looked good, the price was reasonable, and I was prepared to make an offer. I was told by the realtor that the property was still in the name of the deceased parents, held in a long-standing estate and had never been transferred. It seemed in all respects that it should be an easy closing and simply a matter of getting the heirs to sign off their interests in the property. Fortunately the attorney checked the abstract and found 16 heirs who had an interest in the property and the estate.

As I continued my investigation, I discovered that some of those heirs were missing and some were scattered all over the country. Some were married and divorced, some had died, and it seemed impossible to make contact with all of them. None had ever signed off their interest in the property.

And, of course, each and every heir had one-sixteenth interest and ownership of the property. My attorney advised me that if we couldn't locate or we missed just one heir, that heir had a right to come back and claim his or her interest in the property.

I knew it could be done, and I also knew it was the realtor's responsibility to do it. However, at that point I figured it wasn't worth the time and effort it would take, so I passed on the deal.

You can easily understand that under these circumstances you need an attorney to protect your investment interests. There are some states, Florida, for instance, where attorneys don't examine abstracts. Buyers in Florida are forced into hiring a title company, which is costly. Apparently the lobbying group representing these title companies was able to get a bill through the Florida legislature giving them the exclusive rights to abstract examinations. I know. I contacted an attorney's office in Florida and was told I would have to go through a title company. I resisted, but it didn't do any good.

So I ended up doing business with a title company. This did not turn out to be an enjoyable experience. When they completed examining the abstract, they came to me and requested that I sign a statement that there were no suits, judgments, or bankruptcies filed against the property.

I tried to make it clear that this wasn't my responsibility and that it was theirs, and that's what I hired them to do. I had no record whatsoever, other than their word, that there were or weren't any suits on file against the former owner. I presented these facts to the title company and asked them how in the world could I sign such a statement? They didn't answer other than, "That's the way it's done."

I refused to sign that document and the sale went through regardless. I bought this property in Florida and the title company bill was $600, which was absolutely ridiculous. I'd be willing to bet that an office staff didn't spend over an hour to examine the abstract.

And what's interesting, to me anyway, that Florida people think differently and aren't bothered by this absurd charge. Because I own property in Florida, in what I call the "Redneck Riviera," my observation is this: There are two ways of doing business in Florida—the right way and the Florida way.

Protecting Your Assets and Estate

Eventually, if you're in the real estate investment business, you're going to create wealth. And if you make money in the real estate business, you definitely want legal advice on how to protect those assets.

As you start counting up your net worth of equity and investments, you definitely need an attorney to establish a reliable will and a definite, secure plan for your estate. If you have established a fairly large estate, there's no doubt you need an attorney. In addition I suggest including an accountant and an estate planner. I personally included my life insurance agent when I planned our estate.

It's my recommendation to every landlord, and everyone else for that matter, that you establish every legitimate and legal plan there is to keep the government from pilfering your hard-earned money.

When I went to my good friend and attorney for estate planning, here's what I told my attorney, my accountant, my family, and some of my friends.

As I age I don't want a stroke. I don't want Alzheimer's. I don't want to be spoon fed in some obscure nursing home. I don't want to lose my driver's license and my car. But most importantly, I don't want the government to get my money.

Everyone tells me that all that makes sense.

My attorney and accountant said they could help me protect my money, but they couldn't do anything for me with the rest of my requests. I guess that's up to me, and so far I've done the best I could.

Making plans for capital gains takes a great deal of legal advice and guidance. Capital gains simply means that the government is going to get your money. Do everything possible to protect yourself from giving up all your profit in capital gains taxes to the government. Your attorney and accountant can and will provide legal advice on methods of beating the capital gain's tax.

So you see, I do have trust in attorneys and I know they are a necessary part of our business and personal lives. And I don't cast them all aside. Now let's get on with the business of suggesting methods of how to protect your property and assets from legal vulnerability.

Legal Vulnerability

Probably the most important aspect of having good legal representation is the fact that real estate entrepreneurs have a considerable amount of vulnerability. When you've got a mixture and combination of buildings and people and laws, you obviously have a great deal of exposure to liability.

Personal Injury

There are all sorts of personal injury claims that can occur in and on property. Someone could fall on the stairs. One of my tenants slipped and fell on the ice. Fortunately, the insurance adjuster handled the claim. The insurance company paid $5000 even though there was no fault on my part.

Unfortunately, there are times when some of this exposure could lead to the need for legal advice and services. That's the way the business is. However, let me interject something here. In part these types of claims are handled by your insurance company. Make sure your property is adequately insured for personal injury and liability.

Discrimination

I suspect that the primary cause of most landlord lawsuits has to do with the various laws covering discrimination. It's important that you consult your insurance agent regarding discrimination coverage. I consulted with my agent, and he informs me that he is not aware of any type of insurance that would cover overt discrimination.

If you have any questions, a reliable source of information regarding discrimination laws is the State Attorney General's Office. Most states, under the guidance of the State Attorney General's Office, publish free booklets covering the various tenant-landlord laws. In our state the Attorney General has issued a booklet of 41 pages titled "Landlords and Tenants: Rights and Responsibilities." These booklets can provide you with a multitude of up-to-date laws regarding your business.

Lead-Based Paint and Asbestos

Another major legal issue is exposure to lead-based paint and asbestos. Usually these items are included in a homeowner's policy, unless there's a lead-based or asbestos paint exclusion. If that is the case, I suggest adding coverage to the policy.

Above All, Keep Your Attorney Advised

My attorney told me to stress that if at any time you're confronted with any sort of legal situation or expectation, both in your business and personal life, don't hesitate to contact an attorney, preferably one you know and one you can trust. And by all means, keep the attorney posted of any activities regarding any legal action.

My attorney said if you're ever confronted by anyone threatening you in any way whatsoever, simply tell them, "Contact my attorney." End it there. To keep a vigilant eye, you need to know that there are some involved in the legal system who are simply looking for any reason to initiate legal action. I think it's safe to say that there are some individuals in the legal business who are not necessarily looking for justice but are looking for money. You can bet that whenever and wherever there's big money and lawsuits, there will be someone there for a payoff.

Here's another striking fact about laws covering the landlording business. Legislators make these laws. It's no secret that most legislators are individuals who are involved in the legal assemblage.

Litigation

The possibility that you might become involved in a lawsuit or litigation of any kind is quite remote. Even so, there are some concerns you should be made aware of. Even though litigation or a lawsuit is a possibility, this is certainly not something that should discourage anyone from planning a real estate investment business.

From my observation, anyone who has been involved in a lawsuit as a defendant should know that, in all probability, whoever is handling the case will do everything he can do to make the defending party at fault. The entire background of the defending party will be checked and rechecked. This can and will include any and all previous legal action. I can assure you that this will include your driving record, any record of DWI, and any other thing the attorney can dig up. The aim is to ruin one's character and reputation.

They will seek out and discover your financial assets. They will closely scrutinize your property and any other possessions and holdings. They're looking for *money*. Guilt or innocence doesn't matter. What's important is finding what assets can be confiscated. Do you ever hear of a poor person being sued?

Unfortunately, lawsuits are a financial and psychological drain and literally can be heartbreakers. Not only can it break people financially, but it can break their spirits.

What this simply means is this: Greed and avarice work hand in hand. The ultimate goal is the payoff. Money is the driving force that leads to liability lawsuits. It has nothing to do with what's right, fairness, or justice. It has to do with money.

Solution

Operate a Totally Ethical Business

The solution is to do everything within your power to operate and conduct your business and personal affairs totally within the legal boundaries. Also, as we've said before, the courts are not very receptive to a landlord's problems. So, my best advice is avoid doing business with and stay away from the court system whenever possible. And be careful, be careful, be careful.

Tenant's Court

In various counties and some states, there are special courts covering tenants' complaints, attempting to resolve tenant-landlord disputes. Most "tenant courts" allow the judge to issue punitive damages, and "punitive damages" simply means money out of your pocket.

For instance, if rent deposit isn't returned in the specified time, the tenant has a right to take the issue to tenant's court. If the tenant wins, the court will rule that the landlord must pay double the amount of the deposit. That means if the tenant has paid a $600 rent deposit, that tenant will receive a judgment in the amount of $1200. In addition, the landlord can be penalized, depending on the ruling of the court. In some states this can be as much as $200 per rent deposit.

Also, if the judge presiding over the tenant's court is convinced that the landlord acted in bad faith in fulfilling the terms of the lease, that judge can rule in favor of the tenant. Here again, the judge can award punitive damages.

This list of issues regarding bad faith includes just about anything. It can even include unintentional errors, mistakes, and oversights. For intentional errors or lack of management—such as a landlord not repairing a leaky faucet or a sewer drain, or a landlord not providing sufficient heat—the landlord can be held responsible and the tenant can be awarded punitive damages.

 Solution

Solve Complaints before They Become Problems

Make every effort to keep your business from being vulnerable to unattended complaints. Solve disputes before they become legal matters.

Dealing with Death

Here are some important steps to take if death or suicide occurs in one of your rental units.

Step Number One: Call a law enforcement office or agency. That can be the sheriff, police, or fire department. Report the full details of what you know. Let them take over at that point. Keep written records. Protect yourself from any litigation so that someone in the legal profession won't try to turn this thing upside down and place the cause of death on the owner of the premises.

Step Number Two: Refer to your rental application and if possible contact any member of the family. Give them the full details of what you know. Inform them that you have contacted the specific law enforcement agency, providing them with the name and address. Again, keep records.

Step Number Three: There's a good chance there will be heirs and family who will come to you and want the keys and demand to get into the unit right away. That being the case, don't let anyone in until you have been given permission to do so by the law officials.

Step Number Four: When the court gives approval, make sure you know who has the right to enter the premises and claim the personal property. Also make sure that the property can be legally released. When the property is removed, prepare a list of all the items and have that person sign a dated statement that the property was removed from the premises. Make certain, with a signed statement, that you are no longer responsible for this property.

Step Number Five: Do everything you can to have the personal property removed as soon as possible. However, there's this possibility you might have to deal with. The personal property might not be removed on time for you to rent the unit. At this point make every effort to tell the heirs, if there are any, or the court if they're involved, that they have an obligation for this rent. Another possibility is this: The property has little if any value. There's no one willing to remove it from the premises. It's junk. That means when you remove it, you're going pay. What can you do? You're going to have to make every attempt to convince the heirs it's their obligation and responsibility. That probably won't be easy. At this point it's a good reminder that you follow the legal procedure in having the personal property removed from the premises.

Step Number Six: In all probability there will rent due, especially if the personal property is not removed in time to prepare the unit for showing and the issue is closed. Notify the heirs or whoever is handling the estate that rent is due. Do not release any rent deposit until this is entirely settled to your satisfaction.

Step Number Seven: Proceed to collect rent and expenses. The tenant/heirs are legally responsible for any and all current and past-due rent in addition to all expenses in removing personal property and settling the rent deposit. If the estate is probated, submit a bill to the probate court. However, if there is no probate, it might be difficult to get a settlement. Again, inform anyone involved with the estate, family, or heirs, that there are obligations to be settled. Don't hesitate to go after whomever you can.

If that rent, current or past due, is not paid, you might have to take the case to court. Of course, do this only if you know there are assets you can attach if you're issued a judgment by the court. If there are no assets, save your money.

If you've used every effort possible and it gets to the point where there are no assets, it would be my recommendation that you turn the entire procedure over to a reliable credit bureau for collection. They usually have the availability and finesse to handle these cases. It's a lot easier for them to find if there are any assets and let them decide if the case should proceed to conciliation court. At this stage I have a feeling that about all you have left is *hope*—the hope that someone, a relative or a friend, will come forward and settle this obligation.

The Problems of a Suicidal Death

In the case of a suicidal death, there are tremendous problems. If a suicide takes place in the rental unit, there are unbelievable expenses. The number-one question is this. Who is responsible for the cleanup?

First of all, hope, again we're back to hope, hope there's sufficient rent deposit to cover the expenses incurred when a suicide takes place in your rental unit. From what I've heard from landlords, and by the way, this isn't that uncommon, it's doubtful that there'll be sufficient money to cover all the expenses. One of the largest expenses is cleaning up. The cost of cleanup can be an expensive, unforeseen predicament.

I have a friend who had a suicide take place in his rental unit. Here's what he was faced with. The cleanup was almost financially immeasurable. Let's start with covering the expense of blood-splattered walls, carpet, and floor. Just to give you an idea, the person who killed himself, with a gunshot to his head, bled profusely. There was so much blood that it seeped downstairs and flowed into the lower unit. This meant the landlord not only had to deal with cleanup of the unit where the suicide occurred, but also with the fact that the people in the lower unit moved out immediately. This unit too had to be thoroughly cleaned. In order to get the unit back to livable condition, it was necessary to remove and replace all of the carpeting. In addition, the blood actually seeped into some of the wooden flooring, which had to be torn up and replaced. Because the blood literally splattered all over some of the walls, woodwork and plaster they too had to be replaced in both units.

Do you know what the main issue was in the cleanup and inspection? It was the ever-threatening fact that it could be HIV-infected blood. My friend, the landlord, soon learned that in this age of blood diseases, the cleanup couldn't simply be done by just any cleaning service. Any and all possibility of any blood (disease) had to be removed from the premises. It was necessary for him to contact and hire a very expensive specialty company to do the cleanup work. It not only turned out to be very expensive, but it was necessary for him to have this work completed to protect himself from any litigation, now or in the future.

There was obviously insufficient rent deposit to cover these exorbitant expenses. In fact, the cost of the blood cleanup was far more than double the rent deposit. This still left the expense of normal cleanup, removal of property, and past-due rent. The end result was that the owner simply had to pay heavily and chalk this entire episode up to experience and a part of the cost of operation.

To cover the expenses beyond the rent deposit, find out if there's any estate. There will most likely be a family member there to pick up personal property. Check and ask if any of these people will pay the expenses.

Because of the unusual circumstances, you might even consider checking into any government agency, and God only knows there are many of them, that might come to your aid. You just never know.

Solution

I doubt that there is a solution. You can't stop people from committing suicide.

Never Lock Out a Tenant

Under no circumstances should you ever lock out a tenant from her rental unit. Don't change the locks on the doors or windows. The only time you as a landlord have this right is with a court order. If a tenant has been locked out without this court order, she has a right to call a police officer and break into the rental unit.

If a tenant is locked out and can prove that it wasn't done legally, she has every right to file a legal complaint through her respective district court. If this occurs, it could end up costing you the landlord lots of money. For instance, in some states, the tenant can be awarded up to $500 plus reasonable attorney fees.

Dealing with Government Bureaucracies

My additional advice beyond what I've already given before about government attorneys and bureaucracies is this: Stay as far away from all government bureaucracies and government agencies as much as you can. Without irritating them, have as little to do with these agencies as possible.

Don't get into an argument or any altercation with a government agency bureaucrat. If you do, it's a no-win situation and you're asking for trouble. If you violate a bureaucrat or bureaucratic agency in any way whatsoever, they'll come back at you unmercifully. They will stay on your case relentlessly until you either give up, break down, or go broke. You can't fight them.

They are not your friends, so don't suck up to them. In fact, don't even contact them unless you have to. Just stay away from them.

I received the following free advice from a college vice president regarding government intrusion and infringement in our lives. Although it has little to do with real estate, I thought you might be interested in this story.

I asked if the private college was accredited. The vice president said, "No, and the reason that we are not accredited is because we don't want anything to do with any government agency or government bureaucracy. We do not ask for or take any money from the government. Our students are not subsidized by any government agency. If they do not have sufficient income to pay for their education, we pay it ourselves.

We feel that once money is handed over from the government, eventually they will start invading your business and dictate highly bureaucratic doctrine. We know that in order to be accredited, we have to go through government hoops. It simply is not worth it. Therefore accreditation is not that important to us. We graduate our students, and our placement is as good as any accredited college."

Chapter 7

The Rent Application or Application for Lease

In this day and age of lawsuits, and especially those aimed at land-lords, it's important that you establish some sort of program to protect your business and yourself not only from lawsuits but also other tenant problems.

The rent application is a protective device that can help you avoid undesirable tenants, major rental problems, and ultimately, lawsuits.

Every competent employer has a job application. They simply do not hire anyone unless the potential employee completes this form. They want to know what kind of a person they will be hiring. If you've ever applied for a job, you know this.

There is no reason to change this procedure when you're dealing with your personally owned rental property. You have a right to protect that property, just as an employer has the right to hire whom she considers the best. As a long-time investor in real estate, I'm convinced that it's *very* important for you, as a real estate investor, to be concerned about who rents your property.

A job is a job, and the employer can always fire whomever they wish, subject to various and sundry lawsuits. However, it's not that easy to "fire" a tenant. Therefore, you need every protective measure you can use to keep from renting to a tenant who turns out to be a "slug," or one that you can't "fire." It's not that easy in the real estate business.

The starting point of establishing this protection is a rent application or application for lease. Insofar as any law is concerned, you have a right to ask the potential tenant to fill out an application for rent. The applicant, of course, has the right to refuse.

You'll soon learn that if any individual refuses to complete the rent application, it is in all probability one you do not want as a tenant.

That refusal to fill out a rent application reveals to me that the person might be hiding something that they don't want to be known. In all probability, it's usually something you don't want to deal with. There are enough problems to have to solve.

It also tells me that this is an independent individual, possibly a whiner or complainer who could be looking at every angle or opening of a conflict or even a lawsuit. If that individual becomes an entrenched tenant in your apartment, it eventually could lead to more problems than you want.

Somehow or another they try to find any and every possible excuse to irritate you. Just think. A rent application can help give you some sort of method of avoiding this kind of person. Now let's get on with the application. I'm going to do my best to explain to you what each of the items in a rent application is and what it means to you.

After being in the rental business for some 30 years, I can assure you that renting without some sort of protection is foolish and makes no sense. In this age of various bureaucratic regulations that we landlords have to deal with, we need all the protection we can get. Maybe some 10 or 15 years ago it was simpler, but times change, regulations regarding rental property change, and so do people. Not knowing whom you're dealing with and going blindly into a rental lease without some sort of rental application, you just never know what kind of a goofy tenant you might end up with.

Remember: This is a rental application and not a lease. There's a tremendous difference. The rent application is not a binding contract. There are no legal obligations on either the owner of the property or the potential tenant. It is simply an application to apply for consideration to rent the property. This rental application gives you the opportunity to have a preliminary look at your potential tenant. It can give you information that will be very helpful in determining if you want to go further. I will give you enough information so that you can make an all-important decision, one way or another, to rent out your property. It isn't as important or as binding as the lease.

One very important item in the application for rent is that you acquire the legal right to conduct a credit search on the individual. We'll get into more details regarding that credit search in the chapter covering credit bureaus and credit reports.

The lease, on the other hand, is a contractual agreement whereby you make a commitment to rent the property and the signer makes a commitment to rent. There's an entire section on the importance and terms of the lease. So let's go over a rental application.

Start with a Form That Fits Your Needs

Actually, there's no universal or legal rent application form in the sense that it has to be uniform or specific. You can make up your own application. In so doing, you can include just about any questions you want, as long as they are legal.

As we go through this form, you'll see some of the questions you'll ask that will be important in selecting *good* tenants. The only thing to keep in mind, if and when you make up your application, is to make certain that the questions coincide with your respective state laws.

For instance, don't ask about ethic background, religious preference, national origin, sex, race, color, creed, sexual orientation, disability, or reliance on government assistance...welfare. I think it's a good idea when you complete your personalized application that you have an attorney review it. Make sure there's no opening in any way whatsoever that the applicant can come back with some sort of frivolous legal action. You certainly don't need that problem.

There are literally hundreds of people within the legal business who seem to be lurking behind every bush and tree waiting to start a lawsuit, especially against landlords who discriminate. Having said that, let's go through the application item by item. After reviewing this application, you should be able to accumulate sufficient information to make a logical judgment about whether or not you want to allow the individual or individuals to rent your property.

Expect That This Procedure Can Be Time-Consuming

There are some landlords who say that having to go through all this process is somewhat burdensome and time-consuming and they don't want to bother. That might be the case, but the smart landlord will take the time. It might be burdensome and time-consuming, but I can tell you this: The successful landlords use this system, and I recommend that you use the same process.

It will become clear and obvious to you how you can keep from getting stuck with a "slug," a "loser" tenant. I can assure you that you don't want the problem of a tenant who isn't going to pay the rent or a tenant who might create chaos in the building or cause damage to your personal property. These are the kinds of tenants who create problems that you don't want or need.

That, in essence, is what the message is. Use a rental applicaton to eliminate and avoid unnecessary problems. I'll try to give you the information you'll need to screen that potential tenant. As we go through this application, understand that a questionnaire, an application for rent for a potential tenant, is not a commitment to accept that individual. Let's start.

Title

Establish a title for the form. Let's simply call it an application for lease.

Item 1: Legal Obligation

Start your application with the following legal statement in bold print. This is a specific legal item that must be included in the rental application. It basically covers discrimination laws:

**THIS APPLICATION IS FOR EQUAL
HOUSING OPPORTUNITY**

Item 2: Your Name

Furnish your business or firm name or your personal name.

Item 3: Location of Property

List the location/address of the property, apartment, and the rental unit number.

Item 4: Number of Occupants

Ask the following question: How many people will occupy the premises?

Reason: There's an important reason for having the applicant answer this question. Let's say you have a small one- or two-bedroom apartment. If the applicant has several children, the probability is that your apartment simply is not large enough to fit a growing family.

In some cases you eventually can get to a point where the applicants verbally confront you. You can simply tell them in so many words, "I don't believe my apartment has sufficient room and is not big enough to fit your needs."

Sometimes you might get an argument. They'll say, "Oh, I can make that decision, and I think we'll fit in fine." At this point, stand firm. Tell them, "No, this is my decision and I have to make the choice." As you go through the life of an investor, you'll learn that a large family in a small apartment is very hard on the wear and tear of your property.

Rationale: I'm sure you don't want a tenant who's going to move into your building with an elephant.

Rights of Refusal: A real estate investor has rights of refusal. You don't have to take an irresponsible tenant in your property.

Be Cautious: As government bureaucracies go, some states have become more socialistic. I think of California, Minnesota, Oregon, and perhaps there are others. I have a feeling that eventually some of the bureaucrats who obtain this power, through mandated laws, would just as soon have the right to tell you, an independent landlord, that you must rent to everyone and anyone without question. It's seems to be getting closer to that all the time.

Item 5: Names of Applicants

Obviously it's necessary to have the applicants' personal names and social security numbers.

Reason: Always keep in mind that you might be dealing with more than one person, a married couple, an unmarried couple, or even several students. You want everyone that's going to be living in the property to be responsible for paying the rent.

Caution: If you decide to rent to students, they will probably only sign a 9-month lease, or they might sign a 12-month lease, and leave at the end of the school year in the spring. At the end of the school year, they will simply pull up stakes and leave, going back to their home-town for the summer. It can and does happen.

Item 6: Social Security Numbers

Obtain the social security numbers of all applicants.

Reason: It is absolutely necessary to have all social security numbers in order to acquire credit reports.

Item 7: Ages

List the applicants' names with dates of birth.

Reason: You'll find as you get into the rental business that the last thing you want to deal with is a teenager or a young, single, immature tenant.

Item 8: Current Address and Phone Number

List current address, phone number, and, if applicable, permanent home address.

Reason: The permanent address can clue you in and tell you if it's a student. If so, you'll want to know her home address in case, for one reason or another, you have to get in touch with a family member.

Item 9: Vehicles

Have the applicant list the make, model, year, license number, and state of registration. You might also want to include the insurance name and policy number of the applicant's vehicle.

Reason: You'll want to have the right to know, especially if you pro-vide the tenant with parking or garage space.

Item 10: Job Status

Income and financial information, job status, position, and length of time on the job are all important. It might be a good idea to include her supervisor's name and company phone number.

Reason: You never know when you might have to contact your tenant at work, for various reasons. Job status, income, and business information will be very important information for you, giving you the financial factors you'll be dealing with. By having this information in your file, it can save you time later in having to look up how to get in touch with the tenant for whatever reason.

Item 11: References

Then, an all-important part of your application, have the applicant list references. Include with the references the following information:

- Name of bank, address, phone number, type of account, savings, checking.
- Present landlord, phone number, address of property, and monthly rent paid
- Length of time at apartment and reason for leaving.
- Any previous landlords.

Item 12: Crime Report

Do I Have a Right to Ask if the Applicant Has Ever Committed Any Crimes?

The answer is *yes*. However, there's no law that says the applicant has to answer. If it appears to be something that you should check more thoroughly, you might have to do a search through the police department. But if it gets to this point, you might not want to go any further with the applicant or interview. At any rate, on your application form, put in the following question: Have you ever been convicted of any crime, and if so, what crime or crimes?

Item 13: The Credit Report

What Do I Need on the Application in Order to Get a Credit Report?

Make sure you verbally notify the potential tenant that you'll be acquiring a credit report.

You must include the following statement on your application!

In compliance with all the provisions of the Fair Credit Reporting Act I certify that I understand the permissible purposes for obtaining and give Notice that the above named firm or individual may request a credit Report for rental purposes. I have read and understand this contract.

Reason: This gives you the right to acquire a credit report, and this is the most important part of the process of selecting the best tenants. Without that written and signed statement, a credit bureau will not give you a credit report. If the applicant refuses to accept this part of the rental application, you don't want her as a tenant.

Item 14: Signatures

Provide a place for the signatures of all applicants.

That completes the application for a nonbinding lease application. This is your investigation tool, and from that you can proceed to the next stage of screening tenants.

The Next Step

Scrutinize the application. There's a lot of information that's useful and can give you the ability to proceed with your investigation. Start by calling one or more of the previous landlords. Find out why the tenant left. Did she have any trouble with this landlord?

There's no reason to call any of the personal references. You know and I know that no applicant is going to give you the names of people who are about to give negative recommendations.

So far, if things are looking good and you're satisfied that the person or persons are potentially good tenants, the next step is to make contact with your respective credit bureau and order credit reports.

Chapter 8

Understanding the Lease and Contractual Agreement

The lease is one of your more important legal documents. You can make up your own lease to fit your own particular location and individual property. I also would recommend that you contact a print shop or a realtor's office and acquire a ready-made lease. Most of these offices have lease forms that are available for a nominal fee. Get one and you can always use your copy machine.

I also suggest that you check your lease form with your attorney so that you are reasonably sure that it covers some of the dubious laws that seem to overprotect the tenant. If you're attorney is confident that it's a legal lease, you can also verify it through your particular state Attorney General's Office.

If the lease form you receive from your printer or a Realtor has been approved, then be sure the following statement is written on the form:

The (name your state) Attorney General's Office has certified that this Lease complies with the (state) Plain Language Contract Act.

It's significant for you to understand how important a lease is. By having a signed lease, you, the tenant, the fair housing administration, legal aid services, and any legal entity can and will know what to expect. After all, the last thing you want is some frivolous lawsuit over terms of the lease. The following are terms of the lease.

Item One: Names of the Applicants

Start with the residents' names, listing all of the persons that will be involved with the lease.

Reason: Let's say there are three college girls/boys who have applied for and qualify to move into the apartment. What can happen is this: In the middle of the school year, one or two of the girls/boys might have flunked out or decided to move to another location. This event occurs many times during a college year.

If there's only one person who signed the lease, then that person is responsible for the entire lease. What happens if that principal signer moves out in the middle of the year without giving notice? Who then becomes responsible if no one else has signed the lease? What happens is that each one or the other blames one or the other for responsibility for the rent.

However, if all occupants sign the lease, then each of them is equally responsible for the total lease. If one moves out, the others can't just pay their portion and tell you to go after the other person.

Another problem you want to avoid is this: In the event of a divorce, while both parties occupy the property, you want to know who's responsible for payment of the rent if one or the other moves out. If both sign that lease, then each is equally responsible. It's important to be protected from both parties.

In this case, and in theory, both parties become responsible for fulfilling the lease. However, as you well know, when it becomes a legal issue, terms can be twisted in this contract to fit the needs of the client. So this ruling isn't written in cement, but at least you have something to work with in case of a separation or divorce. Usually what I've done is after a divorce, I tell the tenants living in the apartment that whatever agreement they made with their legal representatives and each other is between them, and is not my responsibility.

Item Two: Starting and Ending Dates of the Lease

Reason: At this point you're going to want to let it be known that this lease is from the first of the month and each subsequent month. This means that if the lease reads that it ends on the 30th or 31st of the month they can't move out on the 15th and expect they only have to pay for half the month's rent. This occurs frequently in a college town. When the school year ends or the 7th or 10th of the month, there's no reason for the students to stick around until the end of the month. Then they're gone. If you have this time factor written into the lease, then there's no question when the lease period ends.

Item Three: Financial Terms

Next put in the amount of monthly rent and the terms of rent. State in the lease when the rent is due: on the 1st, 3rd, or 5th, or whatever date you wish on your contract. For instance, if the rent isn't paid by the due date, there's a $20 (or whatever figure you want to use) penalty. Very specifically put in the lease all the expenses that are to be paid by the tenant.

Reason: You must have a total understanding and inform the tenant both verbally and in writing who pays for the various expenses of that apartment or rental unit, and this includes who pays for the utilities, gas, electric, garbage, or whatever. If garages are available and there's additional rent, these terms must be included in the lease agreement. There should be no questions about these charges so that a tenant doesn't come back in a month or two and say, "Oh, I thought you paid for that."

Service charge, i.e., if the tenant writes a bad check they understand it's their responsibility to pay the check and a service charge. In addition, be aware that some banks will charge a fee to you, the receiver of the bad check.

Item Four: Manager-Owner Signature

Next, provide a place for your signature or the authorized manager, or any management firm to sign the contract. Include your name, address, and phone number.

Item Five: Tenant Signature

Following your signature, have designated spaces for the tenant or tenants signatures. Again, keep in mind that you want everyone who is responsible for that apartment or rental unit to sign.

More Specific Terms of Lease

Yes, there's more. The most important thing about the lease is to make sure you cover everything that a lawyer is going to look for and everything that the tenant has to be responsible for. I've written these agreement terms in a universal manner so they are not copyrighted and you have my permission to use them.

Protect Yourself from Any of the Following Problems: Include These Items in the Lease

Financial Agreement

Terms of Payment: Resident will pay the full monthly rent before midnight on the first day of each month while this lease is in effect and during any extensions or renewals of this lease. (If you have an office or permanent location for operating the business, put in here the location where the rent is to be paid.)

Amount of Rent and Method of Payment: Set up terms that the rent is due on the 5th of the month, with a stipulation that if not paid by the 10th there's a $20 penalty and if not paid by the 25th another $20 penalty.

Responsibility for Rent: Each resident who has signed the rental lease is responsible for paying the full amount of rent and any other money owed associated with the rental unit, including rent and damage deposit.

Payment of Rent after Eviction: If any of the lease holders is evicted because of violation of the lease, the lease holder must pay the full monthly rent until the apartment is rerented, or the date of the lease ends, or if the lease is a month-to-month lease. If the unit is rerented for less than the rent due under the original lease, the lease holder will be responsible for the difference until the date the lease ends or if the lease is a month-to-month lease.

Service Charge for Late Rent and Returned Check: The resident will pay the service charge if the full month's rent is not paid by the 5th of the month. Resident will also pay a fee, under terms of the state law, for each returned check.

Use and Occupancy of Lease: Only the person or persons listed on the lease as residents may live in the rental unit. Persons not listed as residents may live in the unit only with prior written consent of the owner or manager. Residents may use the apartment and utilities for normal residential purposes only.

If the owner/management cannot provide the apartment to the leaseholder at the start of the lease, the lessor cannot sue the management for any resulting damages, but the lessor will not have to pay rent until occupied by lessor.

If the lessor moves out before the end of the lease, that resident will be responsible for all rent and any losses incurred, including court and attorneys' fees. If the lessor moves out the date the lease ends the occupant must give the owner/management prior written notice. When the lease ends the management and occupant can mutually agree on a month-to-month lease.

If the lessor violates any terms of the lease, he can be evicted immediately without notice. Any illegal substance, including drugs, constitutes unlawful possession and is grounds for automatic eviction.

Subletting: The lessor may not lease to other persons (sublet), assign this lease or sell this lease without the prior written consent of management.

Conditional Terms: The resident will avoid any and all acts of loud, boisterous, unruly, or thoughtless actions of disturbing the rights of the other residents to peace and quiet, or allow the residents guests to do so.

The resident will use the apartment only as a private residence and not in any way operate anything that is illegal or dangerous or that would cause cancellation, restriction, or increase in premium in management's insurance.

The resident will not use or store any flammable or explosive substance near or in the apartment.

The resident may not keep a waterbed in the apartment without prior consent.

The resident will be given a three-day eviction notice.

The resident will not damage or misuse any part of the rental unit.

The resident will notify the management of any dangerous conditions of safety and health.

The resident will notify the management of any immediate damage that could cause damage to the apartment, except for wear and tear.

Rental Security Deposit: The owner/manager may keep the security deposit for damage to the apartment, other than for normal wear and tear or for any past-due rent owed.

If the apartment is damaged by the resident, to the point of being nonlivable, this lease can be cancelled immediately and the resident will be required to move out immediately.

If the unit damage is caused by elements beyond the control of the tenant and becomes nonlivable, the resident will receive the balance of the monthly rental amount and any rent deposit that is applicable after inspection of the property.

Moving Out before End of Lease: Resident is responsible for all rent to end of lease. If moving out, the resident must notify management, at which time the lease will be reviewed.

When it's a month-to-month-lease, then resident must give a full month's notice of termination. Sometimes moving out before the lease is expired is an unforeseeable occurrence: job status, moving to another community. It's true that a hard-nosed landlord will make the resident live up to the terms of the lease; however, if you're in a smaller community and you want to build a reputation of being a good landlord, you're going to want to try to be as reasonable as possible.

Eviction: The resident can be evicted if any of the terms of the contract are violated. An unlawful act, including drugs, constitutes grounds for automatic eviction. If management must bring legal action against the resident, the resident will pay legal fees.

Right to Enter: The management has a right to enter the property at the time of eviction.

Damage and/or Injury Control: The management is not responsible for any damage or injury done to resident or guests on the property. It is the obligation of the renter to provide her own rental insurance to protect against injuries and property damage. Management is not responsible for any acts of damage or injury by a third party, guests, and/or intruders.

Damage Deposit: *Management* will have the right to pay for any property damage, cost of repair or service caused by negligence on the part of the resident. This will include the cost of removal of resident's property left on the premises.

Pets: Charge an extra $45 per month for in-house pets.

Enforcing the Lease

The lease is a legal document. There should be no reason any landlord would have trouble enforcing the terms of the lease. There could be arguments about various situations, but the tenant must live up to the terms of the lease. Not doing so can become a legal violation.

Chapter 9

Know and Understand the Benefits of the Credit Report

Never Ignore the Importance of a Credit Report

Because this book is designed to help you find methods of operating a real estate business with a minimum amount of stress, and the maximum amount of profit, I want to pass on to you the following statement. I firmly believe that one of the most powerful and important tools you have available as a landlord in screening your potential tenants is the credit report.

The information you receive from a credit report can be a life saver in avoiding rental problems, financial problems, and psychological problems. You realize that you're most likely going to rent your personally owned property to a total stranger, someone you don't directly know and probably barely met. For this reason it's a necessity to at least obtain some knowledge and information about that individual or individuals.

The rent application gives you a great deal of information. However, it's necessary to go beyond that. The credit report can provide you with a great deal of information, and assurance that you're not going to get stuck with someone who doesn't care about responsibility.

I can assure you, most people who don't pay their bills also don't take care of their own responsibilities. The credit report will give you complete information about how that individual pays her credit obligations. But there's a great deal of inferential information in that report regarding the lifestyle of that individual. The credit report can and will reveal character flaws. Let's take a look.

Bad Payment Habits Can Reveal Character Flaws

People who don't pay their bills are obviously an extremely poor credit risk. But what else does this tell us about them? Many things. For instance, when people are careless about paying their credit obligations, they are usually careless about their consideration for other people. If they were considerate, they'd pay their obligations for the services received. And most of these people that don't pay their bills are careless with other people's property.

And for you, the landlord, this means they might not care about their responsibilities, and decide they just won't pay their rent and won't take care of the property. From my experience, they become neglectful, sloppy, careless, and passive about taking care of the property. They don't clean up or fix up; they just use and use the property.

From my experience I've found that if people with bad credit become tenants, it's usually a constant battle trying to get them to pay their rent on time. And it's a battle in getting rid of them as tenants. These people are quick learners, very shrewd operators, and they know how to beat the system.

Most of them have a way of hustling other people. I can assure you that if you rent to people who don't pay their bills, it's just a matter of time before they'll begin the slippery slope of neglecting to pay their rent on time.

Excuses to Justify Not Paying Bills

Once they get behind on rent, they find all sorts of excuses. Here are some of them. The major justification for their credit and financial problems is that those concerns and faults are caused by someone other than themselves. They weep and cry and insist that "It's someone else's fault," not theirs, or "the bank made a mistake." Those individuals who don't pay and don't intend to pay their obligations have a list of excuses for not paying their bills that could fill a book.

Be careful because eventually they can somehow get your sympathy. If you let them get to the point where you start feeling sorry for them, then they've gotcha. Another costly problem in dealing with people who don't pay their bills is that you might end up with the cost of eviction. This is not only costly but also time-consuming. To maintain peace of mind, you don't need this.

My experience both in the credit world and real estate business is that landlords who get caught in this trap end up losers. I've been confronted by some of my landlord friends who did in fact get caught in this trap, even after they had received an insolvent credit rating on the individual.

One of the amazing things to me in the real estate business and the credit business is the fact that somehow or another there are landlords who take on tenants with bad credit, absolutely convinced that they're going to get paid by that deadbeat. I don't know how they come up with this idea, and I certainly don't understand it.

I've had landlords come to me for credit and collection advice once they've discovered they have a deadbeat living in their unit. It's kind of like the old saying, "Once the horse is out of the barn, how do you get him back in?" The damage is done and now they want to know what they can do. Because they know they're faced with a possible financial loss, they ask me how they can make any sort of recovery.

In a nice way, in an attempt to let them know they should have known better, I usually will ask them, "What in the world made you think, after you got a credit report and knew the individual didn't pay her bills, that she would pay you when she doesn't pay anyone else?" (Sometimes landlords try to save a few dollars by not getting credit reports.)

When confronted with this kind of problem, I usually give them the truth and tell them they've been had. They pretty well know. They realize that it's been a financial learning lesson. The simple lesson this: If they don't pay others, they won't pay you.

 ## Solution

Acquire a Credit Report on Every Applicant

I've said this before, and it certainly bears repeating. If you have only one rental unit, it's very important to know the character and credit of the person that's going to rent that unit.

That credit report is one method of protecting not only your income but also your property. To me, it's as essential as any other phase of the landlording rental business. Think of the problems you can save yourself if you can eliminate tenants who don't pay their rent.

The Importance of the Authorization

Before we proceed to the credit report itself, here's a reminder. In order to get a credit report, it's absolutely necessary to have written authorization with the social security number from the individual to acquire the report from the credit agency.

Here's one more word of advice. If that person or those persons aren't willing to give this authorization, it's best to suspend any further communication and go on to the next applicant. Incidentally, in most states it's legal to have the prospective tenant pay a fee for the credit report. However, be sure you check with your state law.

Informaton Provided in the Credit Report

When you become a member of a credit bureau, that bureau will go over the details of the report or reports with you. If not, then use another bureau. The reports are standard and once explained are fully understandable. The credit report itself comes on a plain sheet of paper, is universal, and is printed off a computer. Here's most of the information in a standard credit bureau report.

The Report

Date and Time
At the top of the report page is the first item—the time of day and date the report was ordered.

Name, Address, Phone
Next is the name and spouse's name of the individual/individuals, including address and telephone number.

Social Security Number
Next listed on the report is the social security number.

(Reminder: you must have the individual's social security number in order to acquire a credit report. You can obtain that social security number from your prospective tenant's application for rent or lease. Again, if they're not willing to give this important information, don't go any further with your interview.)

Former Address

The report will include former addresses, the wife's maiden name, and her social security number.

(Having this information and knowing the former addresses can lead you to former landlords for interviews.)

Employment Record

The next item on the credit report is the individual's employment record.

(Often this information is brief.)

Longevity of File

Following is a record of how long the credit reporting company has maintained a file record on the individual.

Accounts for Collection

Next is a list of accounts of various bills that have been turned over for collection and will reveal whether these collections are yet open or paid in full.

(This is an important part of the report. If, from the information in the report, you become aware of accounts for collection, it means the person is careless about paying bills and someone you want to avoid.)

Public Records

Next is a summary of public records. This includes suits, judgments, tax liens, and bankruptcies. These records remain in the credit file for seven years.

(Herein are key factors in determining whether this is a credit risk, or an individual you want to consider as a tenant. Suits, judgments, tax liens, and bankruptcy are items of considerable concern. If there are any of these records in the report, I'd hesitate to rent to anyone with this kind of background.)

Delinquency Records

Following those items the report discloses how many creditors are rating their accounts in the report. This section will also specify if there are any slow payments or delinquencies on any of the accounts.

Credit Pay Record

Following those basic factors is a list of department stores, banks, real estate mortgage companies, credit card companies, car loans, major department stores, and all accounts where the individual has a credit business. Each individual loan or credit transaction is reported to the credit reporting agency, which includes the date the account was opened, the amount of monthly payment and the record and history of payments on the account.

(The information in this part of the report is of great importance. If that individual has a record of paying obligations on time, that's what you're looking for. Does this help determine who the "good" people are? Most likely.

If people pay their bills as they should, in all probability they will pay their rent on time. This part of the report can help to give you confidence that there are good people out there. On the other hand, pay attention to this. If the report shows that they don't pay their bills on time, they most likely aren't going to pay their rent on time.)

Bankruptcy Record

The report will give the date of bankruptcy and a record of how many bills were charged to loss, due to the individual filing bankruptcy.

(The sad story is that I find most of those who lose money on a bankruptcy are small, legitimate business and professional people who are struggling to make things work successfully. That's the tragedy of the bankruptcy laws. They don't take into consideration the victims.)

That bankruptcy record remains in the credit file of that individual for 10 years.

(If a person files bankruptcy, he has to wait another 10 years before filing for bankruptcy again. And do you know something? Most of those same people run up bills, don't pay anyone, and then file again in 10 years.

I find no difficulty in expressing my opinion about anyone who files bankruptcy. It, with the sanction of our wonderful government bureaucracy and court system made up of trial attorneys, has made the bankruptcy laws so easy that it has become a legal method to steal. Most of those who file bankruptcy are thieves in the night, and the day too for that matter.

There are few reasons for anyone to file bankruptcy, and I haven't found many of them. It's simply a case of slovenly individuals out to beat the system. They lie, steal, and cheat. Get them out of here; I don't want anything to do with them and you shouldn't either. Do your business without them.)

A Record of Stolen Credit Cards

If a credit card is lost or stolen, this information is included in the report.

Number of Requests for Report

At the end of the report there is a list and number of businesses who requested a credit report on the individual prior to your report.

Valuable History

That's a tremendous amount of history and information about the individual. This report should give you sufficient information to know if that potential tenant pays her bills on time. That provides a good start and is what you're primarily concerned with.

Don't try to operate your business and attempt to rent your personally owned property without the credit report. The conclusion is this: If they don't pay their bills, you don't want them as tenants.

Don't "Credit Eyeball" a Potential Tenant

Here's some sage advice, and it's kind of like the old saying, "penny wise and pound foolish." There are landlords, and I know some of them, who think they can save a few dollars by not joining a credit bureau and spending a small fee for a credit report. They might get by with this theory for a while, but eventually it's going to catch up to them, and they're going to get stuck with a deadbeat and suffer a tremendous loss.

I can assure you that if you get one individual who doesn't pay his rent, the amount of the loss can far outweigh the small fee paid for credit bureau membership, perhaps no more than a couple hundred dollars, and the nominal amount for a report. If one tenant runs out without paying rent or sticks it to you so that you might have to evict, it will be a lot more than a couple of hundred dollars.

Don't Be Lulled into Passivity

When things are going well and everything is working the way it should, we sometimes have a tendency to become complacent. I even know some landlords who become paternal when dealing with tenants and potential tenants. Beware if this should happen to you. Let me give you some cases in point.

All of us visit and fraternize with friends and business associates on a daily basis. Most of our associates are pretty decent and honest people, and pretty soon we think that everyone is decent and honest. They aren't.

So, in some cases, some real estate investors become complacent. They accept the fact that all potential tenants, because they "look good," are decent and honest. When one interviews that potential tenant on a personal basis, in her complacency she thinks she's got a good person. She's convinced that she'll get paid the rent because that individual appeared to be honest and dependable. That's a way to operate a real estate business in the blind. That's called "eyeballing."

What "eyeballing" a potential tenant means is this. You look at the individual, listen to his story, take everything in as factual and truthful, and decide that he "looks good." You believe he is decent and honest.

So, simply on that observation you make a commitment to rent to him. You do so without having any knowledge of his background and no record of any undesirable credit or record of a negative past history.

There are some of these con-artists who prey on people who trust everyone. Some are just waiting to take advantage of whomever they can. These are the ones to avoid.

These people are intelligent, smooth, and sweet talkers. All the great con-artists have a way about them so that eventually they can talk someone into buying the Brooklyn Bridge. Turn on the news at any time and hear about all the hustlers out there who are working the system.

And then there are other landlords who get a credit report, find a history of bad credit, and still think they should rent to the applicant. They get to a point of being desperate to fill their vacancy. It's hard to understand some landlords' thinking. It simply doesn't work that way.

 **Solution**

Don't Overlook the Credit Report

I've lectured enough on the importance of getting a credit report. You should understand by now.

Chapter 10

Finding a
Credit Bureau

Using Your Local Credit Bureau

As an individual investor, you should have no problem finding and becoming a member of a credit bureau. Here's how to go about it. In order to get the best of service with the least amount of problems, I recommend that you seek out a small, independent credit bureau. There are a number of small, independent bureaus in every state and throughout the country.

As far as I know there are no restrictions in using a credit bureau if you follow the rules set up by the Fair Credit Act. The most important rule is this: In order to acquire a credit report on any individual you must have the applicant's written permission.

In fact, without the written permission from the individual, you will not be able to acquire that much-needed credit report, and without that written consent, you can open yourself and your business to some real legal ramifications. Credit bureaus legally cannot and will not issue a credit report unless you have this authorization. Before we get to the actual credit report, there's a second most important rule and that is this: get a credit report on every applicant.

Small, Rural Community Credit Bureaus

In my book *The New No-Nonsense Landlord*, I have a complete chapter on investing in real estate in a small community rather than a large metropolitan area. In all probability I think you'll find that the credit bureau service in a small community is usually more personal, not only for credit reports but also for other services such as collecting your past-due rent.

In a small bureau you can either call in or walk into their office, identify yourself as a member, and I believe you can receive the credit report without any hassle. In addition, in this age of button-pushing telephone calls, you will most likely have direct contact with the person serving you.

So that you understand what I mean by small, independent credit bureaus, I'm going to list a few of them. This will give you an idea so that you can choose whatever respective community and service will best serve you.

We'll go alphabetically state by state, and I'll only list a few of the smaller community bureaus. This is a sampling of some of the bureaus in the various states. You can also check your telephone directory and probably find bureaus that fit your needs.

Disclaimer

Author's note: I've prepared the following list from each state to serve as samples, and none of the bureaus located throughout the country is being left out intentionally. I've tried to stick to listing the small community services.

Alabama

Credit Bureau of Huntsville, PO Box 27, Huntsville, AL 35804-0027,
1-205-533-9010

Credit Bureau Systems, PO Box 3227, Tuscaloosa, AL 35403-7349,
1-205-345-3030

Alaska

Ketchikan Credit Bureau, 320 Bawden, Ketchikan, AL 99901-6548,
1-907-225-5131

Alaska Credit Agency, PO Box 8890, Kodiak, AL 99615-8890,
1-907-486-6376

Northern Credit Services, 407 Halibut, Sitka, AL 99835-7301,
1-907-745-4755

Arizona

Mt. States Credit Corp, PO Box 12280, Casa Grande, AZ 85230-2280,
1-520-836-8914

Credit Bureau of High Country, PO Box 2140, Lakeside, AZ 85929-
2140, 1-520-368-5660

Arkansas

Credit Bureau, PO Box 423, Forrest City, AR 72336-0423, 1-870-633-2562

Mayfair Credit Service, PO Box 221, Searcy, AR 72145-0221
1-501-268-3501

Credit Bureau, PO Box 388, Stuttgart, AR 72160-0388, 1-870-673-2971

California

Britt Credit Service, PO Box 455, Arcata, CA 95518-0455, 1-707-826-8530

Credit Services Inc., 7445 Topanga Blvd, Canoga Park, CA 91305-0607,
1-760-944-0200

Credit Bureau, Inc., 68929 Perez Rd, Cathedral City, CA 92234-7283,
1-760-770-5515

Credit Bureau, PO Box 7600, Chico, CA 95977-7600, 1-530-342-0132

Bureau of Credit Control, PO Box 5321-Diamond Bar, CA 91765-7321, 1-909-861-1873

Credit Bureau of Imperial Co., PO Box 970, El Centro, CA 92244-0970, 1-760-352-7222

Credit Bureau, PO Box 150, Fairfield, CA 94533-0150, 1-7007-429-3211

Bay Area Credit Service, 50 Airport Prkwy, SanLeandro, CA 94577, 1-510-638-7157

Credit Bureau, 12242 Business Park Dr., Truckee, CA 96161-3327 1-530-587-7551

Colorado

Credit Bureau, PO Box 1303, Alamosa, CO 81101-1303, 1-719-589-2516

Credit Corporation, PO Box 217, Arvada, CO 80001-0217, 1-303-422-8181

Credit & Collections, PO Box 458, LaJunta, CO 81050-0458, 1-719-384-8108

Central Credit, 12211 W Alameda Pkwy, Lakewood, CO 80228-2825, 1-303-989-6222

Connecticut

Credit Center, PO Box 1253, Danbury, CT 06813-1253, 1-203-792-0220

Kason Credit Corp., PO Box 1189, Enfield, CT 05093-1189, 1-860-4999

NE Credit Services, 117 Hartford, Tolland, CT 06084-2819, 1-860-871-2380

Delaware

Capital Credit Services, PO Box 496, Dover, DE 19903-0496, 1-302-678-1735

Florida

Credit Control, 498 Palm Springs, Altamone Springs, FL 32701, 1-407-831-8080

Credit Bureau, Ft. Walton Beach, FL 32547

Credit Control, 400 S 57th, Lake Worth, FL 33462-1659, 1-386-752-0068

Credit Bureau, PO Box 764, Marianna, FL 32477-0764, 1-850-526-3932

Credit & Collection Bureau, PO Box 560855, Rockledge, FL 32956-0855

Georgia

Credit & Collections Bureau, 189 Rogers, Blairsville, GA 30512-8508

Credit Bureau, PO Box 1095, Ellijay, GA 30540, 1-800-606-2254

Credit Bureau, PO Box 579, Milledgeville, GA 31059, 1-478-452-5586

Idaho

Credit Bureau, PO Box 1825, Idaho Falls, ID 83403, 1-208-522-7598

Credit Bureau, PO Box 777, Lewiston, ID 83501, 1-208-743-1525

Credit Bureau, PO Box 1727, Pocatello, ID 83204, 1-208-232-7328

Credit Bureau, PO Box 276, Rexburg, ID, 83440, 1-208-356-9306

Illinois

Credit Bureau, 368 Side Sq., Carlinville, IL 62626, 1-217-854-3228

Advance Credit Reports, PO Box 724 Matteson, IL 60443,
   1-708-720-4000

Credit Bureau, 650 N Webster, Taylorville, IL 62568, 1-217-824-2281

Indiana

Credit Services, PO Box 749, Carmel, IN 46802, 1-317-844-1137

Credit Bureau, PO Box 384, Connersville, IN 47331, 1-765-825-4141

Iowa

Retail Credit Assoc., PO Box 71113, Clive, IA 50325, 1-800-441-9652

Kansas

Credit Bureau, ll35 College, Garden City, KS 67846, 1-620-276-7631

Credit Bureau, PO Box 317, Salina, KS 67402, 1-785-827-8706

Kentucky

Credit Bureau, PO Box 885, Elizabethtown, KY 42702, 1-270-737-3366

Credit Bureau, PO Box 9200, Paduch, KY 42001, 1-270-744-9000

Louisiana

Credit Control, PO Box 90461, Lafayette, LA 70509, 1-337-233-4826

Maine

Consumer Credit, PO Box 37, Brunswick, ME 04011, 1-207-725-8781

Maryland

Credit Management, 15779 Columbia Pike, Burtonsville, MD 20866,
    1-301-989-1392
Valley Credit Service, PO Box 2162, Hagerstown, MD 21742,
    1-301-797-6300
Credit Network, 1901 Research, Rockville, MD 20850, 1-301-838-7000

Massachusetts

Wilson Credit Services, 25 North Main, Fall River, MA 02150,
    1-617-884-9444
Credit Services, Inc., PO Box 9100, Hopkinton, MA

Michigan

Credit Services, PO Box 247, Hancock, MI 49930, 1-906-482-4100
Credit Bureau, PO Box 97, Hastings, MI 49508, 1-616-945-3445
Credit Bureau, 624 Nepessing, Lapeer, MI 48446, 1-810-664-4521

Minnesota

Credit Bureau, 2308 Broadway, Alexandria, MN 56308, 1-320-763-6644
Credit Bureau, PO Box 56, Austin, MN 55912, 1-507-433-7381
Credit Bureau, PO Box 99, Marshall, MN 56258, 1-507-532-2393
Credit Bureau, PO Box 568, Grand Rapids, MN 55744,
    1-218-326-3487

Mississippi

Credit Bureau, PO Box 1529, Hattiesburg, MS 39403, 1-601-582-7181
Credit Services, PO Box 791, McComb, MS 39649, 1-601-684-9585

Missouri

Credit Bureau, PO Box 908, Girardeau, MO 63703, 1-573-334-6044

Credit Bureau, 604 W Broadway, West Plains, MO 65775,
1-417-256-7169

Montana

Credit Bureau, PO Box 1512, Havre, MT, 59501, 1-406-265-7871

Nebraska

Credit Mgmt. Services, PO Box 1512, Grand Island, NB 68802,
1-308-382-3000

Credit Bureau, PO Box 555, Fremont, NB 68026, 1-402-721-2010

Nevada

Credit Bureau, PO Box 29299, Las Vegas, 89104, 1-702-871-6122

New Hampshire

Credit Services, PO Box 6539, Nashua, NH 03063, 1-603-882-8157

New Jersey

Credit Management, 1580 Lemoine, Fort Lee, NJ 07024,
1-201-585-8880

Credit Bureau, PO Box 1006, Old Bridge, NJ 08857, 1-732-679-9100

New Mexico

Credit Bureau, PO Box 21545, Espanola, NM 87532, 1-505-753 7231

New York

Credit Services, PO Box 427, Bath, NY 14810, 1-607-776-7689

Credit Bureau, PO Box 216, Hamburg, NY 14075, 1-716-649-6600

North Carolina

Credit Bureau, PO Box 236, Asheboro, NC 27203, 1-336-625-5524

North Dakota

Credit Bureau, PO Box 1033, Bismarck, ND 58502, 1-701-223-7730
Credit Bureau, PO Box 908, Wahpeton, ND 58075, 1-701-642-5572

Ohio

Credit Service, Inc., 1669 Lexington, Mansfield, OH 44907,
1-419-524-6446
Credit Bureau, 6973 Promway, North Canton OH 44720, 1-330-494-9494

Oklahoma

Credit Bureau, PO Box 1985, Hickasha, OK 73023, 1-405-224-0373

Oregon

Credit Systems, PO Box 948, Bend, OR 97709, 1-541-382-1121
Credit Bureau, PO Box 2702, Grants Pass, OR 97528, 1-541-479-9517

Pennsylvania

Credit Bureau, PO Box 68, Beaver, PA, 15009, 1-724-774-6510
Central Credit, 100 N 3rd, Sunbury, PA 17801, 1-570-286-7742

Rhode Island

Credit Information Bureau, 70 Jefferson, Warwick, RI 02888,
1-401-781-7770

South Carolina

Credit Bureau, PO Box 1051, Spartanburg, SC 29304, 1-864-582-4024

South Dakota

Midwest Credits, PO Box 1088, Aberdeen, SD 57402, 1-605-225-3262
Credit Bureau, PO Box 234, Watertown, SD 57201, 1-605-886-6240

Tennessee

Credit Services, PO Box 561, Dyersburg, TN 38025-0561, 1-731-285-1331

Texas

Credit Bureau, PO Box 2298, Conroe, TX 77305, 1-936-756-7747

Diversified Credit Systems, PO Box 3424, Longview, TX 75606,
1-903-297-0600

Utah

Credit Service, PO Box 3730, Logan, UT 84323, 1-888-446-7029

Vermont

CAFS, LTD, PO Box 6600, Rutland, VT 05702, 1-802-773-7917

Virginia

Credit Recovery Bureau, PO Box 1100, Alexandria, VA 22313,
1-703-548-1000

Washington

Nationwide Credit Inc., 500 108th, Bellevue, WA 98004, 1-770-612-7249

Credit Bureau, PO Box 310, Oak Harbor, WA 98277, 1-360-675-5971

West Virginia

Credit Services, 1100 Charles Ave., Dunbar, WV 25064, 1-304-766-9100

Wisconsin

Valley Credit Services, PO Box 2125, Appleton, WI 54912, 1-920-734-7121

Credit Services, Inc., 333 Bishops Way, Brookfield, WI 53008,
1-262 784-0200

Wyoming

Credit Bureau, PO Box 1787, Jackson, WY 83001, 1-307-733 7344

Credit Service Co., PO Box 1735, Cody, WY 82414, 1-307-587-5050

Once again, I've listed a couple of agencies in each state just to give
you a sampling of available credit services. I recommend that you look

in your own community and find a bureau or service that will best serve your needs.

There are three major national corporate credit-reporting agencies:

Equifax Information Service Center
PO Box 740241
Atlanta, GA 30374-0241
Phone 1-800-685-1111

Experian National Consumer Center
PO Box 2002
Allen, TX 75013-0949
1-888-397-3742

Trans Union Corporation Consumer Disclosure Center
PO Box 390
Springfield, PA 19064-0390
1-800-888-4213

Of the three, Equifax is probably the most reliable. I don't recommend using any of them. Rather, look for a small, hometown bureau.

 ## Solution

Establish a Hometown Bureau

Once you've established a bureau that you feel is right for you and where you can do business, call or go directly to their office. Inform them about your business and the reason you need a credit report, and tell them that you're interested in their services.

I'm sure that 99 percent of the time they'll be cooperative and helpful. After all, their survival depends on their memberships and fees. Ask what services are available to you and also about the various charges.

Usually the bureau will charge an annual membership fee. This can be anywhere from 60 to 160 dollars per year. In addition to the membership fee, there's a charge for the actual credit report. Usually this will be in the range of 3 to 10 dollars. You might say, "Boy, that's a lot to have to pay for a credit service if I only have to use it once or twice a year."

Ownership of One Property: Get a Credit Report

Listen to me. I've said this before, and it bears repeating. If I only owned one property, I would always and definitely join and use the services of that credit bureau, regardless of the charges. I want to be assured that I can get a credit report on my potential tenant no matter what.

I think you can easily understand that a credit report can be considerably inexpensive in comparison to having to deal with a renter who isn't going to pay his rent. The reason for this book is so that you don't have to go through that learning experience. You will learn that the fee and service charge for the credit report will more than pay for itself. Final answer. I highly recommend finding a small credit bureau that fits in with the same community or a neighboring community where your property is located, and use it.

Chapter 11

Repair, Replacement, and Maintenance

The Cost of Hiring Professional Help

When the time comes that it's necessary to hire professional help for repair, replacement, and maintenance, it is my opinion that working in a smaller community makes that hiring process more beneficial. In general, and again it's my personal opinion and experience, it's a lot easier to establish a closer and more personal relationship in a smaller community when seeking the help of a plumber, electrician, carpenter, hardwareman, or general handy man. And in all likelihood you'll find that he or she is more dependable. However, let me add that no matter where you hire help, it can be costly.

As you analyze your predicament, whatever it might be, the first question you should ask yourself is this, "Can I work the cost of repair, replacement, and maintenance into the budget?"

Another question you might ask is this, "If I'm working at my job and this is my primary source of income, will it pay to take this valuable time away from my work, or am I better off hiring the work done?"

If you're a part-time investor and the real estate isn't your principal income, you might ask yourself, "Can that repair and maintenance work be done nights and/or weekends?" I'm sure you know that this method of getting the work done is by all means the most profitable and beneficial.

 Solution

Fight the Profit Drain: Do It Yourself

There are a lot of things you can do at night and on weekends. Here's a list of some repairs, replacements, and maintenance projects you can easily do:

- Paint
- Fix toilet flushing rubber gasket
- Clean carpet
- Mow grass
- Shovel snow
- Clean basement, hallways

In case you need "casual," part-time help, here's an idea that has worked for a landlord friend of mine. This landlord lives in a community where they have what is called a halfway house or drug and alcohol rehabilitation center. These are individuals who have been involved with drugs and are taking treatment and are off drugs. These are men who have gone through the court system for drug or alcohol or related violations. These are not actually treatment houses nor are they confining, locked-up houses. Most of those confined have gone through treatment and are half way through their rehabilitation program.

Most of them literally have nothing to do but sit around all day. Most are confined, by order of a judge, in the treatment center rather than in jail, and are temporary tenants. So my friend contacted the director and asked for volunteers who would like to do work for minimum wages. Most of them are jumping to get out of the house during the day, so there's no problem getting volunteers. In addition, it gives them an opportunity to earn a little money.

From his experience, he has passed on the following advice. "Don't hire two 18, 19, or 20 year olds. Maybe one, but not two. When two get together on the job, they stand around and slough off." He suggested hiring a mature individual. In fact, one of the people my friend hired was a very competent graduate engineer. That landlord told me he has used this process for a number of years with reliable success. He has found that they are dependable and good workers.

Handling Emergency Repairs

What can be done if you get a call in late evening or even in the middle of the night or on a Sunday?

- The furnace has gone out and there's no heat.
- It's raining and the ceiling is leaking.
- There is no hot water.
- The shower is leaking.
- The dishwasher is backing up into the sink.
- The sewer is plugged and sludge is running back into the basement.

These can be troublesome times for a real estate investor and difficult problems to handle. However, as a landlord they cannot be ignored and must be taken care of as quickly as possible. Without giving immediate attention, there's a possibility of losing good tenants. If that tenant does move out he is going to demand that his full rent deposit be returned. I also am sure that if that payment wasn't returned and the tenant took you to court, you the landlord would lose.

Solution

Get Right to It

If the furnace goes out in the middle of the night and it's bitter cold, try to pacify the tenant until morning if at all possible. If not, be prepared to call a furnace repair person and expect it to be costly. Unfortunately, it'll be necessary to call a service person for most of the other previously mentioned problems.

Remodeling

The two most important rooms in your rental unit are the kitchen and bathroom. Keep them in A-l, top-notch condition so you can attract the best of tenants. When I examine an apartment I want to know if I think my son or daughter or daughter-in-law would like to live in this apartment. I ask myself, "Would she feel at home and comfortable if she lived in this apartment, house, or complex?"

The Kitchen

I've often said that if I ever consider doing any remodeling in my apartment or rental unit, I want to start with any remodeling in the kitchen or the bathroom.

So, as you, the investor, analyze your property for renovation, observe the kitchen. Would you feel comfortable inviting your neighbors in for coffee into the kitchen? Your tenant wants to have the same feeling as you do. It's not necessary to invest thousands of dollars into remodeling. It's a matter of taking on some of the simple things first.

For instance, are the cupboards clean? Are they old, brown, and dull? If so, this is a simple and inexpensive do-it-yourself remodeling project. Brighten them up. You don't have to replace them. Paint them a light color.

Another concern in the kitchen is the lighting. Are there good, bright lights? When people sit down to eat or they have company over, do they feel they are in bright surroundings, or a dimly lit room?

The Bathroom

Also, lighting in the bathroom is important. There's nothing more beneficial than a well-lit bathroom. Most people want to look their best, and the bathroom is where they start looking. It seems like when we get up in the morning, we think we look the worst. People want to prepare themselves for the day's activities so they look better than they did when they woke up. Some of us make it and some of us don't. But so what? It makes people feel good to have a look at themselves before they leave in the morning for work. Therefore, make sure there's sufficient light so they can see if they've made themselves ready for the day's activities.

A full-length mirror is fairly inexpensive and is a good added feature. It doesn't hurt unless you don't want to see yourself in a full-length mirror. Regardless, most people like to take a look. Maybe they look and think they can get rid of that bulge or extra layer of fat that shouldn't be there. It can be indicative that they need to get on a diet. And let me tell you something, I'm no great physical specimen when it comes to physical features, but I still like to take a look at myself in a full-length mirror every morning and see if I'm getting fat, older, or falling apart.

Incidentally, when I go to buy a replacement toilet I've found that the "government bureaucratic water-saver toilets" are totally inadequate and deficient. The ones we replaced in our rental units are such that you have to flush twice and sometimes three times in order to make them work. When purchasing a replacement toilet, shop for one that assures you of a good flush.

To help eliminate some sewer problems, which are a common occurrence in rental units, put a conspicuous note in the bathroom: "Please do not flush sanitary napkins or paper towels in the toilet."

The Living Room

Although I'm convinced that the kitchen and bathroom are most important, don't overlook the living room. Keep it clean. Keep the carpet clean, especially of odors from the previous tenant. If need be, take the time to rent an inexpensive carpet-cleaning machine and do it yourself.

I've always thought it's a good idea to keep the living room walls brightly colored, preferably white or off-white. Don't let the tenant paint without your permission and only with your authorized color. Have a strict understanding with the tenant that the painting has to be done according to your specifications. A friend of mine let a tenant paint the living room, and he painted everything in the room that didn't move. That included the woodwork around the doors and windows. And the color was hideous. When that tenant moved out, the entire room had to be repainted.

The Bedroom

I won't elaborate on the bedroom, other than to make sure it's clean, the carpet is clean, and it's well-kept.

Lead Paint, Lead Pipes

The government drumbeat is out regarding lead paint in homes, and of course in apartment buildings and rental units. I suppose someone within the legal aid system sued somebody that had lead-based paint and won a multimillion-dollar judgment. Now that it's in the hands of the government, they've decided that if we don't get rid of lead paint, all 280,000,000 of us will die from lead paint poisoning.

I lived with lead paint in my very humble home for many years. I ate lead paint, I breathed lead paint, and lived in every room in our house next to lead paint, both in the wall paint in our home and in the one lead pipe coming into our home for our water system. That lead pipe went from the outdoor well to the kitchen, and provided us with our water supply. The well was no more than 70 feet from the outdoor two-holer. Incidentally, the water usually froze solid in the winter so we'd use a blowtorch to melt the ice in that lead pipe.

By all supposed government statistics regarding the dangers of lead paint, and it's influence on the bodies of our generation, we all should have been dead 20 years ago. The point of all this is to make you aware that most older apartments and homes (built prior to 1960) were constructed with lead water pipes, and almost all the rooms were painted with lead-based paint, especially the woodwork. That's the way it was. That's all that was available at the time.

You, as investor, must be made aware of this lead threat, especially if you're looking at some of those older investment properties. It is the contention of the government that if children are exposed to objects covered with lead-based paint, the lead can transfer onto their hands and then into their mouths… and ultimately result in paint poisoning and death.

Before buying a property, make sure you know how much lead-based paint is exposed in that building. Sometimes this isn't so easy. Often that lead-based paint has been covered with a water-based paint. Some lead paint can be visually obvious. There are devices you can buy that can reveal lead in property. You'll most likely find lead in older painted walls and lead water pipes.

Contact a paint store or paint contractor and ask if you can legally paint water-based paint over the lead-based paint. If they don't have an answer, check with local laws covering this issue. Another source of a potential problem is lead pipes, especially in older properties.

The information regarding exposure to lead paint and lead pipes must be reported on any real estate sale. The exception could be if you're making a sale to an individual on a contract for deed. Most loaning agencies will balk at giving a loan if there's any lead exposure. Be sure that it's a clear issue before signing any papers.

Mold

Here's a short synopsis of mold. Don't depend on this for a total answer to mold problems you might have. Mold is a fungus created from excess moisture, and people can become sick from mold exposed to the skin and from breathing mold and mold dust.

You can visibly detect mold. And you can also smell mold. Mold smells musty and has an earthy smell. In a home or apartment building, mold can be found near and around a leaky roof, leaking water pipes or hot water heater, basement moist walls and flooded areas.

You'll most likely find mold along sheet rock walls. It also can be found and in and around various sundry materials, like cardboard boxes. I suppose the biggest concern for landlords is that it can be found under carpet. You know what cats do? They urinate, and that moisture not only goes into the carpet but also down into the woodwork below. The moral to this story is have a no-pet policy. To correct contaminated areas, it's important to dry everything. Clean and disinfect the areas. Throw out infested carpet and rugs. Check the plastered walls.

Mold Exposure

Let me tell you my story about mold (we've already gone over the lead paint) in the house where I grew up. In the 1930s and 1940s I lived with my grandparents in a small Midwestern community. We had no running water, no inside toilet (only an outside two-holer), no furnace, and no hot water heater. Our basement was not a basement but a cellar. A cellar is a hole in the ground. The walls were plain black dirt, as was the floor. In the spring of the year when the snow melted, and in the spring, summer, and fall when it rained, the water ran into the cellar and there was often an inch or two of water on the surface of the dirt floor. The house was not insulated, so when it rained, often the rain fell so hard that it blew right into the interior plastered walls. The windows were leaky, and during a snowstorm, the snow would pile up on the interior window ledge, and often into the room.

During the winter on a wash day, all the clothing would be hung inside on racks and rope strung throughout the rooms to dry. The walls, from the wet clothing, were always dripping with moisture.

Did the moisture create mold? I imagine there were various places throughout the house and in the cellar, which was a breeding ground for mold. I don't ever remember anyone in our home or anyplace else that ever talked about the so-called danger of mold.

My grandmother was a neat, clean, and concerned housekeeper. If she had any idea that this mold was such a threat, she'd have burned the house down. I don't even remember using the word "mold" back in those days. We simply lived with it. But do you know something? My grandparents lived in that house, as did I, to a ripe old age, and were never threatened by the mold that was engrained in that property.

If mold is or was such a dangerous threat, my grandparents and I should have been sick or dead many years ago. We weren't. My grandmother died of a stroke and my grandfather, who smoked all his life, died of throat and lung cancer.

Most of our neighbors in that community lived in the same basic conditions that we did, and nothing that I recall in our life was ever blamed on mold. And they want me to believe that mold presents eminent danger to our health?

Enter the Legal Profession

What does all this mean? Is there a possibility that some attorney contrived mold as a health danger and found that it represented money? After hearing about some of the various legal cases, it appears that lawyers have gotten on to something that means big, big bucks. This, the mold scare, will now replace the old asbestos scare.

Mold lawsuits have become one of the greatest boondoggles for attorneys and are a fast-growing business for liability attorneys. It seems like most of the mold fright and legal cases emerge from opportunistic lawyers. I don't know if there's enough proof that mold is such a health hazard. However, I'm convinced that mold suits are no laughing matter.

For instance, in Miami, Florida, an apartment owner lost a case in court and had to pay huge claims to all of the tenants, and go through the expense of cleaning mold out all of the apartments. And to top it off, the "attorney-judge" awarded attorney fees of $3,000,000 plus $300,000 in attorney expenses.

Do you suppose these kinds of things, these unconscionable million-dollar payouts, have anything to do with the exorbitant insurance premiums we pay? Now, we don't all own large apartment complexes. However, we are all vulnerable to legal liability, and it proves that everyone everywhere is held captive to the threat of these mold lawsuits.

 Solution

Avoid Lawsuits

These new lawsuits are so neoteric that they've got us all scared, and there hasn't been a simple solution for landlords. From the study I've done, however, I've learned that there's no reason that you can't remove mold. There are products you can buy. One is called NAS-12, the other No More Mold. The price runs about $10 to $15 per gallon. Both are available at most hardware or paint stores. My only other suggestion is to hire a mold contractor to inspect your property. I did, and it cost $340 per unit. Supposedly the $340 got rid of all of the mold. What next?

Water Savers?

Have you had the same problem with government-sanctioned toilets? Remember when the bureaucrats came out with this great idea that a toilet could be manufactured that would save water. Well guess what? They got their way, and we were all forced into installing "water saver" toilets.

No one I know, homeowners or apartment owners, saved water or money, or anything else. In fact, the saving turned into a colossal expenditure. I put those water-saving toilets in my units and discovered that they take two or three flushes to work.

After the fiasco was exposed, someone came up with a better toilet that didn't take two and three flushes. That meant we had to continue using the "water savers" or replace them with the newer toilets. It's a case of our government "watchdog" mandating untested rules and regulations with no thought of the consequences. These so-called rules and regulations usually end up costing all of us.

Purchase Durable Materials

Although I profess to being a "cheapskate" in owning, managing, and buying properties and materials, there's one area where cheap doesn't necessarily mean better or best. Cheap can often turn out to be expensive. Here are some examples of what I mean.

You can easily purchase an inexpensive stainless steel kitchen sink for about $99. It's adequate, but in all likelihood it won't last for more than two or three years. It then gets stained from soap and water and becomes dull and drab. You can get by, but it has been my experience that if you purchase a $250 sink, it can conceivably last for many years and remain in good condition.

The same applies for shower stalls. A cheap one will function adequately but will not hold up, which means tenant complaints or replacement. I'm convinced a more expensive one should last substantially longer.

If you're going to recarpet, don't put in the least expensive. Shop around for bargains and you might find some high-priced and better carpet on sale. Buy a tough material, although as a novice it's very hard to know what is good and what isn't so good. Don't install white carpeting in a rental unit. White carpet will show dirt and stains immediately.

When renovating or remodeling, there's no doubt you can go to the "marts" and buy cheap materials. But the question is, will they last? Therefore it is my suggestion that you shop for and purchase durable materials.

A Profit Maker—The Duplex

I've always thought that one of the best investments in the rental business is to start with a duplex. Do you know why I say this? Because, as a starter, you establish a home for yourself. You live in one half of that duplex and you rent out the other half. In my mind that's hard to beat. Let me tell you why.

Half of the property becomes investment property and qualifies for tax benefits. You collect rental income from that half. But here's something that's unbeatable. You receive monthly rental income from the one half and that rental income pays part of or maybe even all of the monthly mortgage payment.

But then let me add one more important benefit. As an investor you have an opportunity to renovate that rental unit. Once renovated, you can move in at the point of vacancy and then start renovating the other unit. That means all the money spent for materials and labor are tax-deductible. Think of the financial benefits of this.

Are there some tax benefits? Let's take a hypothetical incident. Let's say a window breaks. You go about your normal business duties of replacing that window. If the repair takes place in the rental unit, then you're legally able to deduct this window as a business expense.

Negative Factors of Using a Management Firm

Usually management firms will charge 8 to 12 percent, and sometimes more, to take care of your property. If you pay 8 percent, you're probably going to get an 8-percent management service, in other words, cheap. Possibly if you pay 12 percent you just might have a better manager. However, let me add that there are no statistics that prove that point.

I believe a primary concern for hiring a management firm is this. Most management firms are realtors and are involved in other facets of the real estate business. Most management firms own rental units and apartment complexes.

You know what that means? I can tell you. It means that if a vacancy occurs in your property and their property at the same time, you know exactly whose vacancy will be filled first. This is probably the one major drawback in hiring a management firm.

The management firms I've visited with also have a complaint regarding investors and property owners. The owners are reluctant to spend money on improvements. Subsequently, some landlords will complain to the management firm that they aren't doing the job of taking care of their property. They call that a Catch-22.

Chapter 12

Developing a Financially Successful Self-Management Program

Seven Steps to Solving Managerial Problems

One question that I'm frequently asked, and a question that most investors consider an area of major concern in acquiring investment property, is this:

How can I be assured that when I buy, own, and manage my investment property that there will be sufficient income from the rent to cover the costs of operation, maintenance, repair, insurance, taxes, and of course the mortgage payment?

From my 30-plus years' experience of owning and managing investment property, I can unequivocally pass on to you the following advice:

If the real estate business and property is operated and managed properly, and if the various problems that each individual investor is confronted with are solved before they become insurmountable, then that real estate

venture should be profitable and should be an enjoyable and
exciting experience.

That's a lot said, and some of you might say, "Yeah, that's easy for you to say. You've already accomplished some of that success. I really don't care about that. What I want to know is how can I be confident that what you have to say will help me in my consideration of investing in real estate or expanding my holdings?"

I can't guarantee anything, but what I can tell you is this. I've used my theories and ideas in this business, and the learning experiences I've had have led to whatever success and failures I might have had.

Although I've read my share of books on real estate investing, I can also tell you I didn't have a book that provided me with at least some direction in solving the various problems that can and do occur in this business. So I worked myself through the anxieties of solving these problems.

I think in all probability that the ideas and theories and learning experiences are worth passing on to others. After all, what good does it do to have all these ideas and not at least share them with someone?

I've said this before. If you take the time to read several books about real estate investing and you acquire one or two good ideas from each book that can create some insights in this business, then it's well worth the time spent.

I'm the first to tell you that what I have to offer isn't going to be totally practical for everyone. But I do feel there's a good probability that some of these suggestions and ideas might work for you and help you in your investment career. Let's start by taking a look at some of them.

Step One:

Start with a Solid Financial Foundation

For anyone interested in establishing or expanding a real estate business, it's important to take plenty of time before making a commitment to buy, renovate, or remodel any property. Take sufficient time to analyze and search out investment property. Don't look at the first property and say, "That's the one I'm going to buy."

And as you shop for real estate, don't get caught up in the hyperbole of realtors. They're out to make a sale. And it's the sale that provides their income. You're probably going to hear something like this from some realtors because some of them will tell you about anything. "If you don't take an option on this property now, it'll be gone in the morning."

Nonsense. If that's the case, tell them you're not interested and let it go and seek out the next property. There are and will be many more. The point is take your time and look at a multitude of properties before making the final decision. It might be necessary to look at as many as 100 properties before you make a final decision. Looking at properties and evaluating them is a priceless learning experience in itself.

Location

If and when you find a property that's of interest to you, and one that you think you can finance and manage, the next step is to thoroughly research the location. What kind of community is it? Do you feel comfortable with the community and location? Ask yourself, "Is this a community where I'd like to live?"

Check the status of the business climate in the community. Is it a growing community or are there signs of business decline? Are there boarded-up store fronts in the business district?

And, of course, examine the neighborhood. Are the neighboring properties in good condition Are there old cars and junk piled around any of the properties? Is there any evidence of crime or drugs?

Is there an abundance of vacancies in the apartment market? Check the "for rent" ads. Take the time to read them. Be sure to consider the vacancy factors in your investment location. Is creeping socialism taking over the real estate market in this community? In some areas the government is entering in and competing with apartment owners and real estate investors.

The next step is checking out the property itself. Let's take a look at some of the problems an investor could be confronted with, especially if an investor doesn't take sufficient time in analyzing all phases of that purchase.

Don't put yourself in a position where you buy a property and discover six months or a year later that you're faced with an astronomical expense you didn't recognize because you didn't devote enough time to appraising and evaluating the property thoroughly.

 Solution

Be Your Own Appraiser First

Before you hire an appraiser, do your own appraising. Go to the property and check the following:

- Is the roof in good condition? A roof replacement can cost thousands of dollars. Make sure it can serve you for a number of years.
- What is the condition of the windows? Are they aged and weather resistant?
- Does the property need painting?
- How is the exterior? Has it been resided with vinyl or steel?
- Is the building well insulated?
- How is the basement?
- Is the foundation sound and in good condition?
- Are the kitchen utilities, stoves, refrigerators, and dishwashers in good condition?
- Is it air conditioned?
- Is the wiring up to code?
- Are there circuit breakers or fuses? Replacement of fuses in a circuit breaker system is expensive.

- Is the plumbing modern? If it's an older unit, are there lead pipes on the premises? (I see some government agencies use the year 1978 for lead paint, and 1960 for lead pipes.
- Is there an asbestos problem? Some of the older homes have asbestos wrapped around heating pipes in the basement. One of my apartment buildings was built in 1927. The entire hot-water-radiator furnace, recently examined and found to be in good condition, is entirely wrapped with asbestos. No one that I know died. However, I have a feeling that when it comes time to sell the property, some bureaucratic inspector will force me to replace the asbestos.
- Is the furnace or heating system in good condition?

Keep in mind that most of these items can cause major repairs or replacements. Most of this is major work and in all probability can't be done by a "jack-knife carpenter." Most real estate investors profess to be "jack-knife carpenters." If you can't do the work yourself, this means hiring expensive craftsmen to do the work. Repairs and replacements cause high material and labor costs.

As you appraise the property, remember that you don't want to be faced with a major expense shortly after you've made the purchase. If you find anything that's particularly alarming, in the sense that it would be a major expense, it might be a good time to back off and continue looking or insist that the seller make the improvements.

If you're fairly new in the investment business, I personally would take one step further and consider hiring a professional real estate appraiser. Good, honest appraisers who look at properties every day can visualize any clinker or any eventual construction problem. They might charge $300 or so, but that can be a good investment. If you hire a professional appraiser, go with that appraiser to the property and spend whatever time you think is necessary so that when you leave you know conclusively that you've made the right choice.

What Constitutes a Good Buy

If you know the purchase price is fair and reasonable, and the rental income of the property will cover the cost of operation, including the mortgage payment, then you should be in a position to say to yourself, "I like it and I think it's a good investment." Incidentally, when I speak of purchasing a property that you think is fair and reasonable, that's all that's important. It's what you think about it that's important.

If you've surrounded yourself with and you listen to advice from negative people, those who say you got a bad deal, then it's time to find new friends. The most important thing is simply to ignore them and don't listen to any of their negativism. What they say is totally unimportant. If you feel good about your offer to purchase a piece of property, that's what's important.

Unforeseen Expenses after the Purchase

Now, getting back to the point of whether the income will support the project. There could be circumstances that can create a financial drain. For instance, if you're faced with some sort of disaster, a fire, or weather-related damage to your property, or if you experience a profusion of vacancies, there's a good possibility that it might be necessary to use your own personal earned income. There also could be a time when you're forced to get behind on payments.

A Financial Sinkhole

Do everything you can to keep from getting behind on your mortgage payments. The added interest and penalties accumulate and create a financial disaster, especially if you don't consult with your banker or mortgage holder. It also can be a major stress factor, something you definitely want to avoid, and a tough problem to solve.

Solution

Contact Your Loan Agent

Obviously some of those unforeseen problems can have a dramatic effect on your rental income. However, if any of these calamities should occur and you don't have sufficient income to make the monthly payment on the mortgage, don't hesitate for one second to contact the mortgage or contract holder and tell them your circumstances. They don't want to become involved in a foreclosure or a bankruptcy and for the most part they'll do everything they can to make this loan work. They will usually work out something on the payment plan, possibly smaller payments or whatever.

Don't give up on the investment. If you've maintained a good financial record with that bank or loan agency and they consider you a good customer, they don't want to lose you as a customer.

For the most part, the banking and loan people are reasonably intelligent and most of them have a heart. I might add that I've found that people and bankers in smaller communities have more heart than those in urban areas. The small-town banker usually can and will be understanding and will try to be helpful. What I've found, again for the most part, is that in urban areas the banks are all large multinational corporations and in my opinion less personable. If the bank where you do business doesn't have "heart," find a new banker. Once again I remind you, no matter where you are banking, when you're faced with a financial crisis, don't hesitate to make contact.

Step Two:

Use Other People's Money

Next, we'll assume you've made the purchase or that you already own rental property. Think of this. The money you're using to make the monthly payment, to build equity, to pay taxes and upkeep, insurance, and maintenance, is not really your money at all. It's the money those tenants are going to bring to your front door or your office or your post office box each and every month. It's "other people's money."

The fact that you're using very little of your own money is one of the major benefits of investing in real estate. And also consider this. Most likely the money you acquired to buy the property was either from the bank or a mortgage holder. So far, it hasn't cost you a great deal, maybe the down payment and closing costs, but you have in fact, so far used "other people's money."

You not only have those benefits, but the government allows the investor to depreciate the property. This constitutes a tax write-off. Now let me add one more benefit. In addition to the depreciation, all improvements and expenses of the property are tax deductible.

Everyone in the real estate business understands "tax write-off." If you don't, your accountant can and will give you complete details and advise you on the steps to take when filing your income tax.

Interest and Equity Building

For the first several years after you buy your property, most of the payment on the mortgage will be applied to interest and not the principal. Building equity in that property and increasing one's net worth takes time. I know of no secret method that creates instant wealth overnight. Well, maybe the lottery, but you know the odds of winning that.

Solution

Be Patient

Simply put, be patient. Eventually the large interest payments will decrease. From that point on, the principal will receive more than the interest. As this occurs, the loan will disintegrate. This represents equity, and equity is what represents net worth.

Here's an example of how building equity and net worth works. Let's say you have a $100,000 mortgage on your investment. Let's also say that the interest on that mortgage is 6.5 percent on a 15-year amortized mortgage schedule. The payment for 15 years is $871.74 per month. Remember, that $871.74 is coming from your tenants. Also remember, the $100,000 you're using is "other people's money" either the banker, the mortgage company, or the previous owner.

After paying $871.74 for 17 months, just a little over 1 year, the $100,000 loan balance is $94,561.75. This represents that after 17 months you will see $5438.25 additional net worth that didn't exist before investing in real estate. In that same 17-month period there's an interest payment of $8509.59 to the bank or mortgage holder. This is tax deductible, and something an accountant will reveal more clearly. The deduction on income tax is money an investor would have paid the government. That's something we all appreciate, keeping the government from taking our money and spending it as they do.

At the end of 5 years there will be a balance of $74,926.23 on the $100,000. That's your net worth gain of $25,073.77. When the 15-year contract is completed, there's a $100,000 increase in your net worth using other people's money. Starting the investment at age 25, at the age of 40 you'd add $100,000 to your net worth. I doubt that you'll find this kind of increase in the stock market.

There's another added benefit. If an investor has taken good care of the property and not let it deteriorate, and if the profit from the rent has been invested back into the property, and if all of this scenario has taken place in a good, growing community, in all probability that property will have increased in value from the original $100,000. That increase, whatever it might be, is an undisputed addition to one's net worth. Once you increase your net worth and build equity, start looking for more property.

Step Three:

Don't Overlook Single-Family Homes

I've had excellent results investing in single-family homes. I'm convinced that single-family homes, if purchased correctly, can be as good an investment as apartment buildings. The key to buying a single-family home is to make sure you don't pay exorbitant prices for that property, and that you invest in a stable, growing community.

I know there are some communities where prices are so outrageously high that it's out of the question to think that you can invest in a high-priced, single-family home and make money. You can't.

I've never been there, but I'd hate to think of buying a single-family home in Los Angles, San Francisco, New York, or Chicago. That too is another subject.

There are some communities where you can invest in a single-family home at a reasonable price. Avoid dilapidated, crime- or drug-ridden, run-down neighborhoods. These are properties you just don't want to own or manage. They too are filled with all sorts of problems, and problems equal anxieties. You don't want to go into this business with a burden of anxieties.

Step Four: Renovate, Upgrade, and Improve Your Property

If all the expenses have been covered, mortgage payment, insurance, taxes, along with general maintenance and upkeep, the next step is to invest shrewdly whatever remainder of the rent money there is back into the property.

Let's look at what can be done with that money. You can make various improvements on the property. Just about anything you do, paint, repair, fix up, will increase the value of the property.

Some improvements that can and will increase the value of the property that aren't all that expensive are cleaning up the exterior of the building, and painting. Probably the least expensive and best method of improving property is keeping carpet clean.

More expensive but highly profitable improvements are installing steel or vinyl siding, upgrading the heating or electrical system, replacing kitchen cupboards, and adding air conditioning,

In theory, here's what's suppose to happen. Let's say in a 10-year period you've put back from rent $15,000. This $15,000 will embellish the value of the property and will increase your net worth by at least $15,000

This also presents an opportunity to raise the rents. Increasing the value of the property and raising rents can in all probability lead to getting the best tenants. That also works.

Solution

Be a Cheapskate

Don't use the rent income for "casual spending" money. Don't depend on using the rental property income for everyday living expenses or increasing your standard of living. Don't use that money for buying a new car. The payments for a new car only add to your financial burden and create more anxieties. New cars create an awful financial sinkhole.

I've seen landlords, especially new investors, who suddenly realize a surge of income from the rent. Some think, "that's easy money," and will start spending it. If they do, they could eventually get themselves in a financial bind.

The moral to this story is that if you wait, all good things can and will happen. The real estate investment business is a patience business. Take the necessary time. Real estate success, despite what the TV pitchmen have to say, doesn't happen in 90 days, and as far as I know there are no get-rich-quick schemes. Carefully manage the rental property and real estate business. Eventually there'll be plenty of personal spending money.

Having established important financial factors, let's concentrate on some of the problems that are necessary to deal with, along with some of the methods of correcting or finding solutions to those problems so the property can and will earn a profit.

Step Five: Do Your Own Work for Profit

In the real estate lingo, its called "sweat equity." And here's how it works. With this plan it doesn't take a great deal of money. The "sweat equity" simply means this. Personally go on the job and do the work.

The type of work I'm talking about consists of small renovation: Repair a toilet or drain, paint, or install carpet. It's time to use self-taught skills. I've often said that a "jack of all trades" is the best kind of investor. A "jack of all trades" doesn't spend money on hiring a repairman or carpenter. It's just a matter of taking the time and doing the work. It works.

Step Six: Avoid Stress and Strain

A concern that everyone in the business has is, "I don't want to 'burn out' and lose interest in my real estate business. What recommendation is there on how I can avoid the stress and strain?"

There's really no simple answer to that. In each and every business in today's society, there's stress and strain no matter what you do. However, there are some simple methods that don't cost anything and can help throttle the stress and strain somewhat.

Solution

Establish and Maintain a Positive Attitude

My first suggestion is this. Establish a good, positive attitude and feeling about your real estate investment business. I'm no physiologist, but common sense says that negativism leads to failure and failure leads to depression and you can't function if you're in a depressed state. Remember you're only dealing with the mind.

Once you get your mind in a negative mode, it's hard to overcome. Suddenly you think you can't do this. Once this occurs, it's time to say to yourself, "It's not true that I can't do it. I can do whatever I want." Make sure you have a positive attitude about yourself all the time, including troubled times. When the positive thoughts start flowing, then you're more easily able to combat the negative. Soon this can and will lead to a pattern and a good habit.

Take time to build friendships and associations with positive people. Look for and become attached to people who are cheerful and who will give you encouragement.

Avoid the whiners, naysayers, and doomsayers. Most of these negative people will drag you down and "beat you to positive-thinking death." They can literally destroy every one of your good ideas.

Now let's take the next step. Let's formulate and understand the positive reasons why any of us are in this dynamic business.

Step Seven: Motivate Yourself

As far as I'm concerned, the prime motivation and the principal reason any of us are in this business, or any business for that matter, is to make a profit and to increase our net worth. And let me tell you, profit and net worth can produce not only positive thoughts and feelings but also peace of mind.

Let's begin by assuming that making money is in fact the motivation and reason you're reading this book and thinking about becoming an investor or extending your investment interests. Incidentally, if that's not the case, that you're not interested in making money, then there's no reason to go any further and bother you with the details, information, problems, and solutions about operating a profitable real estate business.

However, I believe that if you've come this far, I'm correct in assuming that you are interested in making money. I'm also assuming that you are of modest means, probably a beginner investor, and are looking for methods to start buying investment property, or how to make those properties you may already own more profitable.

I would also assume that you are a small investor and that you want to begin this as an auxiliary business and that you do have a primary source of income to live on. Because I'll tell you here and now, I don't have any scheme that will make you rich immediately.

It's important to reinvest the rental income back into the property. And I'm going to take the liberty to assume one more fact. That you are in a financial position that you can reinvest that rental income you accumulate back into your investment property and not spend it on anything other than the property. That reinvestment is a proven money-maker and it works.

Using a Managerial Service

Some of this might be repititious, but it's worth covering again. The first question regarding managerial service is, what fees do these services charge? I've done some research and find that the fee can be anywhere from 6 percent to 20 percent of the gross income.

If your business or occupation doesn't allow you to mange the property yourself, you might want to search for a reliable management firm. One of the major problems in hiring a managerial service is if that service is the owner of rental units, I find it hard to believe they are going to be totally honest in dealing with vacancies. Usually management firms own their own rental units. What's unfavorable about that system is that when dealing with complaints, repair, upgrade, and filling vacancies, the management firm will always be first on the list. I think you can easily understand, and it is my opinion, that they will want to fill their vacancy before showing your unit.

I spent some time with a property manager. I asked, "What is the most difficult problem you face managing other people's property?" He said, "It's hard to convince the property owner to spend money for repairs and upgrading the property."

Problem-Solving in Selling Property: Using the Contract for Deed Purchase or Sale

Don't overlook buying or selling property with a contract for deed. There are, of course, many methods of selling your property. The contract for deed sale will be the only sale we'll discuss. There are some positive aspects of buying and selling property on a contract for deed and there are some negatives. Let's first look at the negatives.

Negative Aspects of the Contract for Deed

Some real estate experts are quite convinced that a contract for deed sale is too risky for various reasons, which we'll go into. No business, no sale, no transaction of any kind in the business world is ever risk free. In all business transactions, whether it's real estate or any other business, there can always be unforeseen problems. That' probably why there aren't all that many entrepreneurs, and there isn't that much competition. Most people are afraid to take a chance.

In the real estate investment business, a contract for deed sale can run into a situation where the buyer has had unforeseen financial difficulties, a bankruptcy, and possibility a death can occur. There's also the possibility of an insurgence of vacancies, creating devastating rental conditions that lead to a lack of sufficient income to make a payment and cover the expenses. As you analyze your potential investment location, make certain that community isn't inundated with vacancies caused by the creeping socialism taking place in the rental business.

Another major weakness in selling on a contract for deed, especially if you're not sure of the financial and credit status of the individual buying the property, is that the owner keeps the rent income for her own personal use, thereby not make any improvements, not caring for the property, and not making the contract payments.

Let me add one more condition that everyone in the real estate business with a sound mind should avoid, and that is taking on a contract for deed sale in a large metropolitan community. The only way for you as a seller to be confident that you won't get the property back in poor condition is to know that there's solid evidence that the individual buying the property was creditworthy and 100-percent reliable, and I mean 100 percent. On the other hand, all my experience has been in a small community where I feel more secure with the contract for deed sale.

A Costly Home Inspection

If and when property is listed for sale with a realtor with a warranty deed transaction, the first step is the necessity of a property inspection. This is a must, and is especially so if there's a loan agency, bank, savings and loan, or credit union financing the sale.

A home inspection gives the buyer an impartial, physical evaluation of the overall condition of the home and lists items that are in need of repair or replacement. The inspection gives a detailed report on the condition of the structural components, exterior, roofing, plumbing, electrical, heating, insulation and ventilation, air conditioning, and interiors.

If the property is not new, it cannot be expected to be in new condition, and therefore the inspector will most likely find various defects. Here's a list of items the inspector will check that will determine the condition of the property:

- Basement
- Ceilings
- Central cooling system
- Central heating system
- Electrical system
- Exterior
- Floors
- Foundation
- Plumbing system
- Roofs
- Wells
- Windows

Here are some of the terms of the inspection:

1. Inspection shall be done by a licensed inspector of the buyer's choice and at the buyer's expense.
2. Buyer and seller shall agree in writing as to whether repair will be performed, waived, or adjusted in the purchase price.
3. The buyer may unilaterally waive defects in writing.
4. Buyer also may declare the purchase agreement null and void by notifying the seller in writing, based on the inspection inadequacies.
5. This is a legally binding contract between buyers and sellers.
6. For any further advice, contact a legal representative.

Here are some examples of problems that can exist after an inspection. Inspectors are especially observant looking for asbestos, lead pipes, lead paint, and mold. Another area of concern is any fire hazard. Here's an example of what I mean. This inspector discovered that there was no firewall between the garage ceiling and the bedrooms above the garage. This of course raises a red flag of concern for the seller, the buyer, and especially the lending agency. Obviously this presents a dangerous fire hazard and extreme liability. This is especially so if children sleep in the bedroom above the garage. Before the sale could be completed, the firewall had to be installed.

In another case, an inspector discovered that there was a suicide in the property. I suppose this could have been learned through various methods, checking with neighbors, or even checking the police report. It didn't create any problem in completing the sale; however, the information had to be reported in the disclosure form and passed on to the buyer.

On a warranty or financed sale (and not a contract for deed), at the completion of the inspection, all the defects are recorded on the disclosure form and then legally signed by the hired inspector, the realtor if there's one involved, and the seller. Then a copy of the disclosure is turned over to the buyer and the financial institution. The cost of a normal inspection is anywhere from $200 to $400, and I wouldn't be surprised that there are some locations where this could be higher.

The next step is negotiating the terms of the sale between the buyer and seller. The question will be "who pays?" That means either the buyer accepts the defects and does the repair work, or the repairs must be corrected by the seller. Most likely, the financial institution will not accept a transfer of the property until the defects are corrected. As these defects are discovered, the next step of repair can become costly.

The Benefits of the Contract for Deed

I've laid out some of the various problems that occur when dealing with a contract for deed. Now let's look at some of the positive aspects t of a contract for deed sale. With a contract for deed sale, the inspection process is eliminated, which means the sale does not have to be inspected and approved by any government agency, city, county, or state. A contract for deed is a legal transaction between two persons, the seller and the buyer. The terms of the sale are private. When the contract for deed sale is completed, it's not necessary to record the deed. However, let me caution you, I highly recommend doing so. And here are the reasons why.

If that contract is not recorded in the respective court house, the buyer can go to a bank and mortgage the property. This means the bank will have a first mortgage ahead of your contracted for deed. If, on the other hand, the contract for deed is recorded, usually the bank will not give a loan or demand that the contract for deed be paid off. When it is recorded, your rights are first.

The recording fee is about $20 to $50, and this fee can vary from location to location. At the time that the contract for deed is recorded, there is no deed tax on a contract for deed transfer. The deed tax is paid only when the contract for deed is completed and the warranty deed is filed. Actually, the contract for deed sales can go on and on through different owners.

Another benefit with a contract for deed sale is that there's no need for a realtor to become involved. With a contract for deed sale, you don't have to pay capital gains tax other than on each monthly payment and not on the total of the sale. The benefit of selling property with a contract for deed literally can save hundreds of dollars.

Of all the 34 properties I've owned, off and on during the years, 90 percent of those I've purchased and sold were on a contract for deed. During that time I had only one negative experience. This occurred back in the era when bankers were charging 21-percent interest. My buyer was forced into bankruptcy because of paying high interest on other properties he had purchased and financed through various banks.

The negative experience I had was that the attorney representing the bankrupt buyer notified me that I had to return several months' contract for deed payments to the bankruptcy court. I did this. However, my attorney made certain that the property was returned to me. On a contract for deed sale, if the payment isn't made as agreed, the property can be confiscated immediately, which we did.

I came out ahead because I had received a down payment, and two years' payments on the contract. Most of this was applied to the 9-percent interest, with just a small amount applied to the principal. The individual involved in the bankruptcy signed a quit claim deed and transferred his interest in the property back to me. I eventually resold the property to the next buyer at the same price, again on a nine-percent contract for deed. Eventually that second buyer, after paying on the contract for deed for several years, refinanced his property and paid off my contract for deed. I used the money and bought a Florida condominium. (I mention that here because it is my opinion that right now and in the foreseeable future, a hot real estate market is recreation property located on any body of water.)

I have also found that of the 34 properties I sold on a contract for deed, 34 eventually refinanced the property and paid off the contract before its due date. During the period of time I held the contract, I was receiving nine-percent interest. So each and every one was a wonderful profit maker in my investment program.

Another financial benefit in selling your property on a contract for deed is that it can be a quick sale. It's not necessary to go through the bank; it's not necessary to get involved with closing costs.

A contract for deed can be a great wealth builder. Usually the seller can and will receive a higher rate than the current bank rate of interest. The money you make on the interest in all probability will equal the amount you paid for the property in the first place.

Solution

Know the Buyer

Let's start with a couple of simple but interesting statistics. First of all, keep in mind that 50 percent of the people are dumber than the other 50 percent. I'd be skeptical in doing business with that lower 50 percent. Another statistic is this. Thirty-three percent of the people are out to cheat and deceive as many people as they can. Definitely avoid this 33 percent. Therefore, the primary concern when selling your property on a contract for deed sale is that you *must* know the people buying the property. You not only have to know them on a personal basis, but also their entire personal history.

An absolute *must* is to have full knowledge of their financial status and most importantly have a clear and concise record of their credit reliability. It's a *must* that you know the buyers to be very responsible, honest, and trustworthy individuals, and know well ahead of time that they will be making the payments as agreed. In addition, you want to know that there's no doubt they will take care of the property. How does one go about establishing this security?

Back to the Credit Bureau

First and foremost, without any doubt whatsoever, this, the contract for deed sale, demands a thorough credit and character investigation. That credit report will give you an indication of the credit and character of the individual you're doing business with. I can tell you right up front, if that person has any blemish in her credit record, this are a warning flag that you should be careful. In my mind, any blemish is enough for me to kill the transaction.

If that individual has any record of past judgments or suits, if that individual filed bankruptcy even *once*, that's warning enough to end your relationship. From my experience, both in the credit business and the real estate business, I've learned that if those people have cheated other people by not paying their bills, they will probably cheat you. It is my opinion that you should avoid these people like the plague.

Individual versus Corporate Ownership

The Advantage of a Limited Liability Company

These are major legal issues and I hesitate to give any specific advice. I can advise you that you should contact some legal representation before establishing a corporation. It's a must. There are some advantages in establishing a corporate ownership or limited liability company. Therefore you should seek legal counsel with an attorney of your choice.

Chapter 13

Creeping Socialism in Real Estate

Enter the Government

One of the real threats occurring in the real estate business is the intrusion of government agencies providing subsidized housing. This is becoming a serious problem for all of us in the rental business. Over the past several years the government ownership of housing of all kinds, individual homes, town houses, and apartments, has become a strong and powerful competitor for all independent real estate investors. The various government agencies that work through a maize of bureaucracies have become giants in this business. It is becoming not only the real estate investor's competition, but an outright nightmare for some investors as they experience more and more vacancies.

Government apartments and homes are subsidized and financed by and through various government bureaucracies. In fact there are so many of them it's hard to track them down. However, I'll make an attempt to tell you how it works.

159

The most interesting part is that they are taking our money, taxes from our real estate, and financing these housing units and creating a market that is virtually impossible to compete with. Do you know why I say this? Because they literally deal with bushel baskets full of money, while we depend on our rental income to support our business operations.

Originating Point: Government Body and Members of Organization

It all starts in your home community. Usually the city council will appoint a committee to investigate the feasibility of acquiring federally subsidized real estate funding. This committee is established quietly and without anyone knowing or even in a position to question what's going on, and most landlords I know don't even know this is taking place until it's too late.

Establishing and Naming the Original Organization

This new community organization is probably called something like City Housing Authority. The organization can include citizen volunteers, but almost always includes a city employee or employees. Often it can be the city attorney, a council member, or the city assessor.

This is the beginning of a community government-subsidized real estate venture. The first subtle subsidization comes when we realize that these city employees are paid by city salaries. What does this mean? It means, right from the start that your tax dollars are being used to create your competitor.

Land Acquisition

The land itself is usually part of the preliminary plan. The city uses tax money to purchase land. The community then presents its plan and proposal to a regional office.

The regional office is staffed with all government employees. They take each individual plan from each community and begin the process of establishing whether that particular community is eligible for housing money. I've never been there, but I'd guess that there aren't too many plans that are turned down. It's another case of jobs. Keeping busy keeps jobs.

Who Has Authorization for Making Contracts?

Usually this authority comes from the regional office, although I assume that it has to be approved by some higher bureaucracy.

Architectural Planning

I've been told that at this stage the regional office calls for bids for the architectural plans.

Approval of Hiring Contractors and Building Materials

I've also been told that all contractors and suppliers of building materials present a bid on the respective projects. The first point of inquiry starts at the local city assessor's office. They provide the basic information of how to proceed for rental units. The staff at the city assessor's office is paid by the city out of city real estate taxes, taxes collected from apartment buildings and contractors who build private homes.

It's been very difficult to follow the money trail of these government-subsidized properties. Most of the money originates in Washington, DC and is funneled through various channels. Most of the money spent for the property is authorized through bids from the various construction companies. The income from the rentals is used for maintenance, and if there isn't enough, the local agency can request more money from the Federal Housing Administration.

The problem for the real estate investor is that it has come to the point that it's possible for just about anyone anywhere to move into either a subsidized home with minimal down payment or a rental apartment with low rent based on income.

In one of the agency brochures it states, "housing that's affordable to all kinds of families." Do you know who they're referring to when they say "All kinds of families?" They are referring to our renters, or I should say, our former tenants.

Let me give you an excellent example of what I mean. In one community, students, who have a limited income, if any, and who formerly were our tenants, qualify for residency in government-subsidized apartments. Do you also know what this means? It means that in some of these college communities, there's going to be a shortage of tenants.

These government houses are financially subsidized. And when bureaucrats take charge of any project, money is never a problem. In the government housing I've observed, whenever there is money needed, they requisition funds, and there they are. Whenever the apartment or townhouse or home is in need of repair or they need to upgrade the property, the respective government agency simply contacts another of the many other government agencies, usually the Federal Housing Administration, and requests more money. This new money is usually granted, almost without question, and is used for maintenance, repair, and upkeep.

It appears, for all practical purposes, that each respective housing authority presents its budget. This includes expenses for operation and salaries for employees, and most of those agencies literally receive money by the "buckets full." That's the same money you and I depend on from our rental income. That's tough to compete with. It's difficult to find any community where some government agency or another hasn't entered into the real estate rental and sales business.

 Solution

Avoid Getting Caught in This Trap

Everyone should be aware of what is occurring in their respective communities. How do you know? As you search for investment property, make a thorough review of what's happening in that community. Check the want ads regarding vacancies in the privately owned apartment units. Those want ads in the local newspaper will tell you a lot. If it's filled with "bargains" and special "deals," such as the first month's rent free or other deductions, it can be an indication that there are too many apartment complexes and it might be a warning sign that the government has saturated the market.

As you investigate communities, check on and know all about the various government agencies that are in the rental and real estate business and how much property they own. Not only should you know what government properties there are, but also find out what's happening with future plans for expansion in that community.

Almost every village, community and city has subsidized housing. For the private investor, it's a matter of knowing how much and whether or not they've saturated the market. Government-subsidized housing is tough competition. They don't have to depend on breaking even with the rental income. In fact, most of the housing units don't depend on making a profit. And they are using taxpayer money, our money, to build those homes and apartment complexes.

You know, I talked this over, the problem of government interference in the rental business, with a number of apartment owners, real estate investors, and rental agencies, and they all agreed that it presents a situation that everyone should be aware of. They know and realize that it's difficult to fight and deal with any government agency. They always seem to have the upper hand. Do you know why? Because they have an endless barrel of money.

Facing this kind of competition, what can be done? Everyone I talked to pretty much agreed that in order to be competitive in the business, and keep their own business growing, in all probability

 it would take some drastic steps. Here are some ideas that might help solve this problem.

Improve Your Property

If you've already made your investment in a community where the government has moved into the apartment and rental business, you're going to have to take steps to secure your tenants and keep pace with the market. The first step is to keep your "house" in order. Once again, as I've stressed before, make sure your property is in A-l condition.

A second step is to consider remodeling, updating, and improving the property. Remember, that kitchen is a number-one room that tenants look at. Make sure your apartment or rental unit is the best. Make sure that it's not getting tacky and run-down. Most work in the kitchen can be done without hired help. Do it yourself. One apartment owner I talked to said that adding a dishwasher can be an advantage.

Start a Rent Price War

The third step, which is somewhat drastic, is to start a price war. Think of it this way. Let's say you've got a four-plex with rents of $500 a month. Now if two of the units are vacant, that's a monthly deficit of much-needed rent, and you're going to be out $1000 each month. What do you do?

You might have to adjust the two occupied units; lower their rent to equal the rent you're going to have to charge to fill vacancies at a lower rate. Whatever you do, don't charge less for a new tenant than those who are already there. The older tenants can and will learn that you've rented for less than what they're paying. You can count on it. The word will get out that their neighbor is paying less rent. The minute they learn this, there's going to be grumbling and confrontation. Some will in all likeli-

hood give notice immediately when they realize they're being snookered.

Another suggestion might be to hold a meeting with other landlords. I don't see them as direct competitors, so I would think they'd all be in favor of giving and exchanging ideas. And a final suggestion—seek out other investment properties.

Chapter 14

Insurance Coverage

My attorney and my insurance agent emphatically told me this: Do not operate your business without having complete and adequate insurance coverage. There's one more fact that I insist on stressing and one I've always believed in. Operate your business totally within the specific laws of your state. Don't even think about taking any chances with your property and your tenants and your reputation by being inattentive, careless, neglectful, thoughtless, or lazy.

Don't be foolish and think you can get by doing something that is even marginally against any of the various business and real estate laws, especially the very vulnerable discrimination laws. In this everchanging world of laws and lawsuits, you can't be too careful. Taking chances isn't worth whatever gain you might think you can attain.

Disclaimer

Insurance is a very important component of an overall real estate business operation. Attorneys love insurance companies. As a matter of fact, insurance companies are literally the lifeblood of most law practices.

Having said that, I was advised by my attorney that I should not provide legal advice regarding insurance coverage, either property insurance or personal insurance. At this point it's necessary to inform you that I don't have the expertise to give advice about insurance coverage. This is a specialized field that requires professional guidance.

 **Solution**

Establish a Reliable Agent

However, there are a few basic commonsense suggestions, non-legal suggestions, that might be helpful as you make decisions regarding insurance coverage on your property and yourself.

Suggestion Number One: Consult with a reliable local insurance agent. Present your entire investment plan with that agent.

Suggestion Number Two: I think it's prudent to establish yourself and your business with just one reputable agent. I believe that if you write all your insurance with that one agent, she should take care of your interests. If not, get another agent.

Suggestion Number Three: There are a lot of insurance companies out there writing insurance, and there are some who aren't all that trustworthy when it comes to paying claims.

As I discussed this issue with my attorney, here's what he suggested. It's mandatory that you know for sure that the company writing your insurance is a trustworthy, dependable, and reliable company. He said there are some companies that can be and are controversial when it comes time to settle claims and pay for losses. They like the premiums, but they are not all that keen about paying out money. He informed me that there are some insurance companies, and he included in his comment some of the large national companies, who will not accept their responsibility, will dispute, and will fight to the end when it comes time to settle the claims. He said they can literally wear you down.

To make sure you are with a reliable company, depend partially on your agent. I say partially because sometimes agents don't know or aren't aware of the reputation of the company. Therefore he suggested that if you have any apprehension about the agent's knowledge of the company or if you have any question about the company, contact your state insurance commissioner. That office will have record of all complaints against companies.

Suggestion Number Four: Protect yourself and your property by having sufficient insurance coverage. Don't think that you can cut costs of operation by underinsuring property.

Mandatory Notification

Suggestion Number Five: Once again, my attorney informed me that whenever you are involved in any claim of any kind, most insurance companies make it mandatory that you contact them immediately. He went on to say, "Don't try to keep the company out of the claim and think you can take care of it yourself."

He said, "If you bypass the company and make an attempt to handle the claim yourself, in all probability the company can and will void your coverage." Therefore, if at any time a claim should occur, let the insurance company adjuster complete the investigation. There's no need for you to get involved. That's why you buy and pay for insurance.

Rent Loss Insurance

If your building is shut down due to a loss (fire, wind, or whatever), it's a good idea to have rent loss insurance. This means the insurance company will pay either a portion or all of your rental income during the time the building is unoccupied. Check with your insurance agent for this coverage.

Tenant Insurance

Include an addendum in your lease that tenants must have tenant insurance. In the lease make sure that the tenant understands that if a loss occurs, you cannot be held responsible. As a landlord I think it's important for you to make sure that every tenant has sufficient renter's insurance. This insurance should include personal liability in case of their own negligence. It also should cover fire damage and loss of personal property, furniture, and clothing.

Probably the landlord isn't responsible for covering any loss. However, if the loss, whatever it might be, is taken to court there's a good possibility the judge could rule in favor of the tenant, even though she didn't have her own insurance.

If nothing else works, consider this. If the tenant doesn't have insurance and there is a small or reasonable loss, it might be best as a landlord to work out some sort of settlement between the two of you rather than ending up in the hands of attorneys.

Million-Dollar Liability Policy

Make sure you understand the difference between a personal policy, an executive policy, and a commercial umbrella policy. Each covers different phases of a business operation. My agent informed me that there are policies that can be $1,000,000 and up to almost an unlimited amount. Of course, he said, the higher amount increases the premium substantially. I get the impression from him, and this was an estimate, that a $1,000,000 policy probably will have a premium of $400 per year.

Solution

Before making any decision, contact your agent for complete details. My attorney highly recommended the million-dollar or two-million policy. He stated that this covers liability gaps that your principal policy doesn't cover. He also recommended that you write this million-dollar-or-plus policy with the same company as your other insurance.

If the property is in your personal name and there's a major claim through a lawsuit, the claimant's attorney can go after any and all of your assets. That million-dollar-plus policy gives you some assurance of not being totally wiped out.

Some investors recommend titling each individual property into a separate corporation and not one individual corporation. For instance, building one could be ABC Corporation, Building One; the next could be ABCD Corporation, Building Two, and so on. That way if there's a claim against that specific property, the loss can only apply to that property and corporation and not your other assets and other corporations. Most of this becomes a legal issue, and you should consult your insurance agent and/or attorney before making a final decision of whether this fits your needs.

Chapter 15

Eviction and Collecting Past-Due Rent

Rent Is the Lifeblood of the Rental Business

Unless you're a wealthy landlord, everyone in the rental business depends on the rental income to support and sustain the investment. It's the rent that pays for general maintenance and upkeep, and it's the rent that provides the monthly mortgage payment. These are the basic facts of survival in the landlording business.

Dealing with the Current Tenant Who Is Past Due

First let's discuss the current tenant, one who usually pays on time but becomes a temporary problem by being past due on rent. Let's say this is the rent that should have been paid by the first of the month or the fifth of the month or whatever time is called for in the terms of the lease. But for some reason or another the tenant just didn't make it.

Sometimes it happens. Some people, at the end of the month, run over their budget and they're short of money. It could be that they have to pay their car insurance premium, or their car broke down and is in need of costly repairs, or any other circumstances that put a stress on their budget. They just don't always have the rent money in on time.

Most tenants in this position feel sheepish and find it hard to justify what they've done. They seem to come up with various excuses about why they don't have the money. They might say things like, "I just don't have the money right now," or "I had an expense I didn't anticipate," or some such thing.

When you, as the landlord, are confronted with this situation, you just have to be up-front and tell them, "I'm really sorry but that's a problem you must solve. It's something you have to work out yourself. I must have the rent money because I have to make the mortgage payment."

Don't hesitate to inform the tenant that the rent is due on the date that is specified in the lease. If the rent isn't paid on that date, there's no grace period. Actually, a landlord can terminate the lease the following day and start eviction action if need be. However, that's the extreme case and it's most likely more harsh than you want to be. In dealing with a comparatively good tenant, in all probability you're going to want to save that tenant, so eviction at this point isn't necessary.

Late Charge

In dealing with late payments, make sure there's an addendum in your lease informing the renter that there's an additional charge, a late fee, when the rent isn't paid on time. The amount of the late fee can and will depend on your area and community. Most landlords I've asked charge $20.

I might add here that it's specified in the lease that there's an additional charge for returned, insufficient-fund checks. Fees for insufficient checks should be more than $20. Most banks now charge you a fee for accepting and depositing that check in your account…believe it or not. Again the amount of the fee can be determined by your area and community.

If a good renter gets behind on rent and it's someone you don't want to lose, your first concern should be to get along with the tenant as well as possible under the circumstances. However, don't become too friendly. If you do, you put yourself in a susceptible position for that tenant to take advantage of you.

Solution

Work It Out

So, if that good tenant gets behind, what do you do? Obviously your first concern is that the rent be paid. Make every attempt to work something out that's satisfactory for both you and that tenant. But don't lose the fact that you need the rent.

A first step is to establish communication. Make personal contact, preferably in person, but if that's not convenient at least by phone. Inform the tenant that you have been satisfied with him as a tenant, but let him know the rent must be paid on time and that it can't happen again.

If this doesn't get immediate results, the next step is send a reminder that the rent is past due. Make sure you call attention to the fact that there's a $20 late fee. If this gets no response, then take the next step.

Now give them a sad story, one similar to what they've given you. Inform the tenant that you understand their circumstances but you have the same problem. You have a monthly payment to make that is totally dependent on the rent. Here's what I'd tell them, "Under no circumstances can I miss even one mortgage payment. If I do, there are late fees and added interest, but more important this reflects on my credit rating. I'm sure if that payment isn't made, the bank is going to call me and they're going to be very firm about getting their payment."

You Are Not Their Legal Guardian

Rent Comes First

For some reason or another some tenants think they can ignore their rent. You have to inform them that they have to realize and establish their priorities. When I make contact with tenants that are not up to date on their rent, I tell them, "Your housing should be number one on your list of obligations. You can miss a car payment, you can miss credit card payments, or any other bill, but your home should be your number-one priority. You don't want to lose your home, therefore you can't ignore paying the rent."

I also let tenants know that I am not their guardian and cannot be responsible for their financial problems. I usually suggest that when they get into these kinds of financial difficulties, they should seek financial help from a family member, their parents, some relative, a friend, or whomever they can get the money from.

Don't string them along even for one month. If they get behind one month, pretty soon it's two months. Once you reach the point of their being two months behind, then it becomes a problem. And this is the kind of problem you want to avoid and you don't need. It's stressful.

If after a month you haven't received any sort of response, other than promises and excuses, then it's time to take the next step. Send a letter to the tenant informing him that you will be running an ad in the paper, "Apartment for rent." In the letter state that you want to know when it's convenient to show the apartment to the next tenant.

If that renter is serious and wants to remain in the rental unit, this will get results. If all that doesn't work you might have to give some thought of eviction. But don't wait too long. Before we get to eviction, let's work on what to do and how to collect past-due rent when it becomes a collection problem, especially if the tenant has moved out.

Solution

Go Back to Your Credit Bureau

When you reach the point of having to collect past-due rent, remember you're in the real estate business and not in the collection business. It is my opinion that you shouldn't waste any valuable time trying to collect past-due rent. It's more important that you spend your time managing your property and taking care of your good tenants. Let someone else do the collecting.

By now you should be convinced that it's a wise move to join and use a credit bureau. If you've taken my advice and done so, in all probability you'll find that the bureau will have some sort of collection service that goes along with your membership. Pay for a membership in your local credit bureau. Work with them.

Here's how some credit bureaus provide collection service for their members. First of all, if you've become a member and paid an annual membership fee, which can be anywhere from $60 to $125 per year for most small bureaus, that membership will include what is called a precollection service. This means that if you turn your account over to the bureau for collection, they will send out one or two letters on their stationary notifying the debtor that the account has been turned over to the credit bureau for collection. At this point the debtor is notified that this account will become a part of her credit file.

Usually the charge for this precollection service is included in your membership fee, and if the bill is paid in the precollection letter, there is no charge. Then if the account isn't paid in the specified time, maybe 15 to 30 days, the account becomes a collection item. At this point the bureau will charge a fee for collection, which could be anywhere from 25 to 50 percent of the total bill. If they do collect the past-due rent account, I've always said that 50 percent of something is a better than a lot of nothing.

There is one final step you might want to consider before filing the account with the credit bureau. Send a letter demanding payment of all past-due rent in full. State in the letter that you will turn the account over to the credit bureau for collection if the account is not paid in five days.

After five days, then take the account to the credit bureau. Don't just sit back and wait. If you do so, it becomes a false threat and the tenant doesn't take you seriously. Turn it over immediately.

On the other hand, I recommend that you eliminate the five days and take the account immediately to your credit bureau. I think the five days in most cases is a waste of time because you're dealing with an irresponsible individual. Look to the credit bureau. Most credit bureaus have a built-in system and the machinery to do collection work.

Most credit bureaus are lucky to collect 33 percent of all the accounts that are turned over for collection, including past-due rents. Do you know what this means? It means that your odds of personally collecting any past-due rent aren't all that good.

Let's look at a situation where a tenant has moved out owing a month or two or however many months of rent. What do you do?

Most credit bureaus will attempt to collect the account through phoning and correspondence. If it isn't paid in a fair amount of time, the credit bureau will check the individual's credit and if there are assets, primarily a job, or ownership of property that can be confiscated through a court order, they will file the account in conciliation court.

Most credit bureaus will pay the conciliation court filing fees, which can be as much as $100 to process the account through the complete court and collecting process. The debtor then is charged back for the fees.

In a great many cases your account will be one of several on the same individual, and the account will be filed jointly with the others. The credit bureau will in all probability charge 50 percent for collection of the account if they have to take legal measures. If the individual has moved out of the territory, the credit bureau can forward the account to another credit bureau for collection so it doesn't become a dead account if she has moved out of town.

An additional feature in dealing directly with the credit bureau is that the past-due rent account will become a part of the individual's credit history and credit record as an unpaid account for collection on his credit report. If the tenant applies for a credit card or a bank loan, or any credit, this is reported. For the most part, the banks will inform him that he must pay the accounts for collection before the bank will advance any loan.

As I said before, statistics show that most Credit Bureaus are only able to collect 33 percent of the accounts turned over for collection. So don't expect miracles and don't expect to get your money the next day.

Once the account is in the hands of the credit bureau, go on to bigger and better things. The main thing is you don't want the burden and anxiety of trying to collect the account.

The Use of Conciliation Court to Collect Past-Due Rent

Conciliation court is also known as small claims court. The purpose of this court is to provide a means for individuals in the rental business, and other businesses for that matter, to solve disputes. For the landlord this covers rent disputes, damage deposit, failure to pay, and eviction problems.

Most small claims courts allow listing of accounts less than $7500, depending on the specific state. The major benefit with small claims court is it is not necessary to hire an attorney. Anyone can file claims. In some cases attorneys are not allowed to enter into small claims.

Filing a claim in small claims court can be an expensive procedure. You pay the filing fee up front, which is $60. That can be more, depending on your location. This $60 is added to whatever amount you've filed, and if you win the case the defendant pays all the charges. Even though you might win the case in court, you are still responsible to collect the money; the judge does not collect your money. Therefore, if you decide to use the court on your own, make sure you recover all the court costs, and there are many.

The sticky part of handling the claims on your own is that you can spend the money to move the account through the court system and you can win, but you only win a judgment. This can be a monetary judgment for past due-rent or for damage to the property or an eviction judgment. You still have to follow through and proceed with an execution against the person. You pay the fee to service the judgment, which can be $70, and mileage to have the sheriff serve the execution.

You also must provide for the sheriff or whoever serves the execution what property you want confiscated, wages, savings, or whatever property you can acquire that is available and not exempt. If there is nothing there, you will have invested a great deal of money, possibly up to a couple of hundred dollars, and still have nothing.

In general, landlords don't have a great record of acceptance by judges in conciliation court. For some reason, it seems from my experience that most judges look at the "rich" landlord versus the "poor" tenant, regardless of who is right or wrong or even the various circumstances. The point is, don't expect too much in these courts.

This, by the way, is especially so when it comes to filing for returned rent deposit. My experience has been that somehow or another that judge just seems to believe the tall tales the tenant has presented in court, despite the fact that there's no proof.

In court make certain you have your facts correct, and have as much visible evidence as possible. For instance, include itemized damage receipts and pictures of unkempt or damaged property.

Separation and Divorce

What happens if a married couple separates while they are dual tenants in your property? Who becomes responsible for past-due rent? Both parties, if they've signed the lease, are responsible. It is not up to you as landlord to make a decision if he or she owes the rent.

When you try to collect the rent, you must have that lease signed by both parties, and then both are responsible. When you call to collect the rent, the one party will tell you that in the divorce decree the other party is responsible. Attorneys will argue the point, but the divorce decree has nothing to do with the lease both signed, which means each is responsible.

The Legal Method to Evict

The first legal step to take in conducting an eviction is this. If that tenant has broken terms of the lease or rental agreement, has been involved with drugs, has been a disruptive tenant, has not paid the rent, has refused to leave the premises, has damaged the property, has pets in violation of no pets allowed, there are steps you can take before becoming legally involved through the court system.

Once you've presented the problem, whatever it might be, the simplest method of eviction is asking/telling the tenant firmly that you want him to voluntarily leave the premises. Confront the individual or individuals on a personal call. Don't become belligerent or hostile and don't get into an argument. If you do, you'll immediately get into a losing battle. In your conversation be firm and insist that you want them to leave the premises immediately. Often this does work and they know they're in trouble and leave.

Offer a Cash Payment before Evicting

The next step is this. The main thrust at this point is to get the tenant out of the unit so you can rerent the property. That tenant is broke. If not the rent would have been paid. So there's a possibility that money will talk.

What I'm now suggesting is costly but in the long run might save you time, money, and anxiety. Offer that "no-good deadbeat tenant" cash. I'm also reminding you that once you analyze the circumstances, you're going to be better off financially if you do this rather than fight it.

Here's why. Hiring an attorney and going through the eviction process can cost up to $1000 just for attorney fees. This doesn't take into consideration other expenses. An eviction can cost another month without rental income. And after an eviction, there's the burden and expense of bringing the unit up to rental condition for the next tenant.

And there's one more consideration. I know of a case where the tenant got an eviction notice and in his anger he literally tore the rental unit apart. You could be faced with this possibility.

Money Talks

Consider offering that tenant money. This can include total return of their rent deposit plus $100 cash (your personal money) or forgiving all the past-due rent and $100. Or whatever offer you might think necessary to get him out. At this point don't try to save money. Don't be too cheap.

Words of Caution

When making this offer, if they agree to the terms, you must have them agree to a firm stipulation that they leave immediately—that they pack their bags and furniture and personal items right now, right there in front of you. Whatever you do, don't hand over any cash or make any sort of financial agreement until the tenant has totally moved out and you have all the keys in your hand. Incidentally, once your business of removal is completed, immediately change the locks. If you give them cash before they move out they might not move out, and believe me, they'll spend your cash.

Once you've established an agreement, have the terms in writing. State specifically that you have returned the tenant's rent deposit or forgiven any past-due rent and rewarded the tenant $100 (or whatever deal you've made) with the agreement that the tenant would permanently leave the premises. And have the tenant sign the document.

Reluctantly and Willingly Hand over the Cash

Now it should be final. Make sure the tenant has totally moved out with all his possessions. He has turned in the keys and you've established an agreement on paper that he is totally satisfied with the terms and will not return to the unit. Now you can give him the cash.

No Results? Start the Process of Eviction

If all that doesn't work, the next step is to start the procedure of eviction immediately. Send a registered letter. Also send a copy of that registered letter by regular mail. Sometimes these people know that a registered letter means trouble and the deadbeats know enough that they can refuse to sign. By sending the regular letter, you have proof that the letters were sent and they were aware of its contents. Send out two letters, one regular mail and one registered mail.

Once the letter has been sent and the tenant calls and wants to talk about it, don't discuss any part of the eviction. This will only lead to an argument, which could end up in a lawsuit. In the letter advise the tenant of the reason for eviction. State, if this be the case, that there have been complaints regarding the disturbances in the property or that you're aware that there are drugs on the premises, or whatever the cause of eviction. In that letter state firmly that you want them to leave the premises immediately. If not, you will contact your attorney and start legal eviction action. In all probability the tenant knows that letter isn't enough to force her to leave, but on the other hand this starts the process, and for the time being is the least expensive method to get him out.

Just about the time you think things are going badly, they get worse. If there's no reaction from the registered letter, the next step is to contact your attorney. He'll advise you on what steps to take.

I'd recommend having the attorney send a letter notifying the tenant that you want him to leave the premises immediately, and if not, you will proceed with a legal eviction. However, if that doesn't produce results and he doesn't leave, it might become necessary to go through the legal process of eviction, which, regardless of the circumstances, still takes a court order. This can become costly—in most locations probably a couple hundred dollars for the court costs plus the attorney fees. And it's time-consuming.

In the process, as the case is presented to the judge, usually that judge will notify the individual that they have 24 hours to leave the premises. If, within that 24-hour period the individual doesn't leave, notify the sheriff, who has the legal right to remove the individual immediately. There should not be a charge for the service of the sheriff.

Evictions are messy to say the least and are hard to deal with. They wear you down. The odds are that you won't collect any rent from any evicted tenant. Once you get to a full-fledged eviction, you can count on the fact that once you evict or even notify a tenant that you intend to proceed with eviction, he's going to turn on you. He will become belligerent and boisterous and blame you for everything.

If the tenant has the potential of eventually coming around concerning some issues such as past-due rent, you might send a notice that the tenant has to correct the problem or he will be evicted. In the letter inform the tenant that he has two weeks to remove himself and all his property. State in the letter that he has violated the lease, and give the reason for the violation. One factor is this: If you plan the eviction for nonpayment of rent and he is on a lease rather than a 30-day rental period, if they pay the rent up to date, you can not enforce the eviction.

Terms of Eviction

1. Landlords cannot in any way forcibly remove a tenant.

2. The landlord must have a legitimate reason to evict the tenant. What are legitimate reasons?

   Not paying the rent.
   Breaking terms of the lease.
   An incident where the tenant simply refuses to leave after notice was given.

3. The landlord must file a complaint against the tenant in court and the tenant must be served with the summons. The sheriff usually does this. The landlord assumes all the costs until the case is ended and judgment is filed against the tenant.

4. A court hearing must be held at which time both the landlord and tenant will tell their stories.

5. The judge makes the decision. The judge can rule that the tenant must leave and a law officer can enforce the ruling.

6. Here's a caveat: If the tenant can show reasonable hardship, the judge can give the tenant another week in which to move.

7. Another caveat: If the eviction notice is for past-due rent, and the tenant pays the past-due rent, he can remain in the premises.

8. If the tenant wins by insisting that the unit was in disrepair, the judge could rule that the rent is abated or reduced either partially or completely.

9. In most states, only a law enforcement officer can physically evict a tenant. A landlord cannot do this.

10. In the case of drug eviction, if at this point nothing has worked, you can legally contact the police. The police have some jurisdiction and under some circumstances can give notice of eviction.

Eviction for Illegal Activities

The law is on your side, and the best method of dealing with illegal activities, especially drugs, is to call the police immediately. If a tenant is engaged in any of the following activities, she can be legally evicted:

1. Selling, making, possessing, purchasing or allowing illegal drugs, on the premises or elsewhere.

2. Illegal possession of firearms.

3. Harboring stolen property.

4. Prostitution.

Special Note: In some cases, if eviction is a problem, it's a good idea to check your state law and have full knowledge of what you can do legally. I say this because in some states the landlord can be held responsible for illegal activities on the premises. The landlord can even be forced to forfeit the real estate, especially with anything having to do with drugs. And if you're not satisfied, and don't really know what to do, don't hesitate in contacting an attorney.

Eviction References

The next question is this. "If I evict a tenant, and that tenant goes to another landlord, and that landlord calls for a reference, what can I tell her?" The facts. If the tenant was evicted, that's a fact. If the tenant lived a lifestyle that didn't satisfy you the landlord, that's a shaky fact.

In giving verbal information about the tenant, evicted or not, and it had to do with other factors, state the paying record, which is a fact, the dates occupied, and the reason for leaving. You can also reveal how many past-due rent payments were made and how many notices you had to give if the rent was past due. Those are facts.

On the other hand, you don't want to get into a position where that future landlord can sue you if you didn't give him adequate information. Even though you might have had a bad experience with the tenant, other than the verifiable facts, he has given you as a reference. Don't get into a causal conversation and reveal things that can haunt you. Don't turn that interview into a legal "rat's nest."

If in the conversation you think you might be skating on thin ice, you simply tell the individual, "If you need more information, you'll have to contact my attorney." Another answer could be, "I've been advised by my attorney that anything I say about that tenant could give him cause to take me to court for defamation of character." Any landlord with an ounce of brains should understand these simple statements. If not, she shouldn't be in the rental business.

A hypothetical case could be something like this. Let's say there was a drinking problem. If you don't have police records to back up the information, drinking can be a hard "fact" to prove. That's the kind of information I personally would hesitate to pass on. If that tenant decided to sue for defamation of character, those are the kinds of things some in the legal profession would like to hear. You know that drinking information, without proof, would be hard to prove in a court of law.

Protect Yourself with Records

Obviously at this point it's important that you do everything you can to protect yourself. When you have an interview with another landlord, keep notes that include dates and all the pertinent information you've passed on. Once you've given the factual information then let the other landlord make his own decision. End the communication at that point.

I can't say enough about how attorneys can literally ruin a business financially. They can and will. Although attorneys can and will often bend the truth, they can also make a lie appear to be the truth. Attorneys get rich on defamation-of-character cases. What's the old saying? "Ninety-nine percent of the attorneys make the 1 percent look bad." And above all, be sure you have adequate insurance to cover your total business as well as your personal operation. Seek out a good insurance agent.

Avoid an Eviction Problem You Don't Need

Here are a couple of examples of evictions you want to avoid. This landlord, someone who would be considered a religious provocateur, rented a house to an individual. Soon after the tenant signed the lease and moved in, he had his girlfriend move in with him, totally unbeknownst to the landlord. This arrangement was very upsetting for the property owner. He contacted the renter and told him could not live in his house if they were not married and that if he didn't voluntarily move, he would be evicted.

The tenant refused to move. Using Civil Liberty attorneys, the tenant took the case to court. The case ended up in the State Supreme Court. The court ruled in favor of the landlord and that the home owner had the right to evict the tenant on the basis of the landlord's religious rights rather than the statute of human rights.

By the time the case was settled the tenant had moved out...for other reasons, so the decision was moot. However, this is an incident important enough to tell so that landlords can be made aware of the various kinds of laws and rulings that can occur in the rental business.

The next unusual eviction case is this. I asked a landlord the following question. "What is the most difficult problem you have ever had to deal with troublesome tenants?" Here's the answer he gave me.

"I own eight family rental units located in a working-class neighborhood. Over the past several years I've had to call the police on numerous occasions because of marital conflicts and family fights. In addition to tenants calling me about these problems, I get calls from the police."

"At first I thought these problems could have and should have been handled by the police. However, what I found out is that they simply 'talked' to the tenants and didn't pursue it any further. Frankly, the police got talked into not taking any legal action. Passive resistance."

(Author's Note: This is a case where the owner didn't take the time, check the credit report, and thoroughly screen the tenants with an application before making a commitment to rent the property.)

Anyway, he went on to say, "Eventually I saw that the police didn't help. I guess in all probability there wasn't much they could do without a court order, and there wasn't that much more I could do without the police assistance. After a while, when it became a persistent problem for me, I finally got disgusted with what the police were able to do, so I took it upon myself to evict these troublemakers as I saw fit."

"The police spent time talking to the people, telling them to settle their family disputes and try to get along with one another."

"There were times when I'd get a call from the police about the family fights and complaints. I'd go right out to the rental unit and listen to the story, but by that time the couple knew they were in trouble and they'd say, 'No sir, there's no trouble."

"I had a number of calls in these units. Eventually I got sick and tired of the same old story. If it was a second or a third call to the same apartment, when the police left I told the tenants very assertively that I wanted them out and I meant business. That usually got results."

"If in a short period of time they weren't out and if there was no one home I'd back up my trailer, load up their possessions and haul it out to a rental storage unit or the dump ground. Then I'd lock the doors so they could not get back in."

I asked that landlord, "Did you ever get sued or have any legal problems with your evictions." He said, "Only once. I got a call from an attorney who said the tenants wanted their property back. I told him where it was and they could pick it up. I also told him they (the tenants) were nothing but a lot of trouble for me and I wanted them out and got them out of my apartment. I also asked for my past-due rent. I didn't get it, but I asked anyway."

"I think the attorney knew they (his clients) were a pack of trouble so he didn't pursue it any further once I told him where and how they could get their property back. I don't know if it would have been that easy if it had been a legal aid government-paid attorney."

Dubious Eviction

I suppose you could say that the landlord broke about every law in the book in proceeding with this kind of eviction. He had no right to go into the apartment, but he did anyway. He had no right to confiscate their property without a court order, but he did anyway.

He had no right to evict them without going through the procedure to do so, but he did it his way anyway…and got by with it. He was lucky. Stupid, but lucky.

Chapter 16

Moving Out
and Rent
Deposit

Don't Overlook the High Cost of Moving Out

I've consulted with cleanup crews about the various work that has to
be done in a short period of time when a tenant moves out. This is
especially so when a tenant has left a proverbial mess in the rental
unit. That cleaning crew told me it's not all that simple and it entails a
lot of work to clean some of these rental units once the tenant leaves.

They've provided me with some information on the best way to clean
a vacated apartment or rental unit. Start in the kitchen. It usually needs
the most attention. Next clean the bathroom and then on to the other
rooms. Leave whatever has to be done with the carpet to last. They said if
you clean the carpet first, you might have to go back and clean it again.

The primary and most conspicuous untidiness is usually in the
kitchen. The former tenant will marginally clean out the stove and
refrigerator. However, there's usually some trace of leftover food, such
as a partial bottle of milk and/or particles of various food products.

The cleanup crew informed me that one of the most time-consuming jobs is cleaning a refrigerator. The next unit that needs attention is the stove. There's usually grease around and under the burners, in the oven, along the crevices, and food particles that have dropped under the stove and out of sight to most observers. Usually the kitchen cupboards haven't been cleaned thoroughly.

The next problem area that takes an unexpected amount of time is the bathroom. The sink, shower, and bathtub have some residuals of dirt and scum and that have never been thoroughly cleaned. To give you an idea of what I mean, one of the cleanup crew members I talked to said in one unit it took an hour and a half just to clean the bathroom.

Pet Cleanup

One of the most undesirable cleanup chores is dirt and impurities left over from pets. Even with a no-pet policy, pets have a way of entering and living full time in the premises. When the tenants and the pets leave, there's always an odor and a certain amount of uncleanness. Usually the renter doesn't detect this because she's lived with the animal and the smell all the time she's been there. So she leaves and the odor remains. It takes some cleaning skill to get the odor eliminated.

The biggest problem is the fact that it's not uncommon that the pet will have urinated on the carpet. This requires a thorough cleaning, or often it means replacing the carpet. Sometimes the flooring has to be replaced.

There can be occasions where there are holes in the walls obviously in need of repair. When the tenants are on the doorstep, ready to leave, they will often confront the owner, manager or landlord and insist, often by not being truthful, that this so-called mess to clean up was not their mess. They'll often say it was that way when they moved in and they'll have a list of all sorts of excuses and supply various causes of the problems. Again, once they are done, they want to go…and want their money back.

Solution

Check the Unit

Once the tenant has finalized his cleaning, don't let yourself get caught in an overwhelming expense when a tenant moves out. What can you do?

Post a Moving Out Notice

It's a good idea to post a MOVE-OUT notice in a conspicuous place in the rental units. This notice can be placed in a plastic cover and put on the side of the refrigerator or inside a kitchen cupboard.

Here's a list and a protective notice informing the tenant that she has these obligations to fulfill before leaving the premises and before any security or rent deposit is returned:

1. Contact the phone, cable, electrical, natural gas, and post office with your new address.

2. Clean the following thoroughly:

   Stove, oven, and burners
   Refrigerator
   Cabinets
   Sink
   Floors
   Bathroom
   Windows
   Closets

3. Garbage removed.

4. We will contact you regarding showing the apartment.

5. Set up time for inspection.

6. Leave forwarding address for refund after inspection.

7. Moving out time noon the last day of the lease.

Despite the fact that this notice is conspicuous, there are good tenants who often become thoughtless when leaving and don't do a thorough job of cleaning up. They get in a rush and want to move on. There can be occasions where this could lead to some belligerence on the part of tenants. At this point their prime concern is to get their rent deposit back and get out. But your leverage is the ever-present and important rent deposit that you want to put on hold until everything is finalized.

Time to Leave

Have an addendum or clause in the lease stating specifically the time of the expiration of the rental agreement or lease. Rather than having the tenants move out at midnight of the last day, state in the lease that they have to be out by noon of the day the lease expires. And of course that certainly doesn't mean noon the next day after the lease is expired.

You the landlord have to be explicit about the moving and timing factor. No matter how well that tenant might have cleaned, you want to be sure that the unit is ready for showing to the next tenant. It's necessary to prepare the unit for the next tenant, so allow yourself enough time to get the work done. The best method is to stipulate in the lease that they must be out at 12:00 noon the last day of the lease. 12:00 noon means 12:00 o'clock.

When tenants give notice, there are times when they say they're leaving on the 30th or 31st of the month. 30th or 31st means 30th or 31st. When the lease is expired, that means the end. That doesn't mean noon of the next day or two days from the end of the lease, but it means the end. If they aren't out at 12:00 noon on the 30th or 31st, inform them specificallly that there will be an additional late charge deducted from the rent deposit. One lost day can mean the difference of an entire month's rent.

Avoid Losing a Month's Rent

There's an urgent need to prepare the unit for the next tenant, which should be your most important, immediate project. As you can tell from the previous comments from the cleanup crew, unless you do it yourself, it can be costly.

A great concern for most landlords is the loss of a month's rent because of inadequate notice given by the tenant. For instance, some tenants will contact you on the 15th of the month and say they're moving out on the 30th, giving you 15 days' notice. Tenants are obligated to give a 30-day rental period notice of intention of leaving. That does not mean they can come in on the 15th and tell you they're leaving the 15th of the following month. It means from the 30th to the 30th (or 31st, whichever applies.)

When the tenants give 30-day notice, it's time to pursue renting the property to the next tenant. Ask the present tenants if it's all right to show the rental unit before the expiration of the notice. They don't really have to give permission to do so, but if you've had a good relationship, they should be agreeable.

Rent and/or Security Deposit

You as a landlord undoubtedly are going to be confronted with one of the most disputed claims that we have to deal with in the business. That's the rent deposit. Tenants want their money and they want it right now, and they want all of it.

Maintain full control over that rent deposit. Don't give out any money until everything is settled. You should expect to be paid for damages that have occurred beyond the normal wear and tear on the property.

It's best to make every effort possible to settle this touchy issue because in some cases the rent deposit can even end up in court. Protect yourself. These are legitimate, legal, and justifiable deductions that you as the landlord must be reimbursed for:

1. Past-due and unpaid rent.

2. Repairs for damage.

    (These repairs must be considered damage beyond the normal wear and tear. Take pictures. These pictures can become an important factor in your claim.)

3. Unpaid utilities.

4. Penalties.

When and if you do end up in court, unfortunately, from my experience, most of the judges favor the "poor" tenant and not the "rich" landlord as I've said before. If you get to this point, have plenty of evidence, which includes specific dates and pictures of damage.

Don't allow the "moving out" tenants to expect that it's their right to use their rent deposit to pay part of the last month's rent, any past-due unpaid rent, any penalties, or their obligations of lights, phone, and other utilities.

Inspection of Property

When the tenants give notice, make arrangements for inspection of the property. If there is damage, call it to their attention. It's important to immediately state the damages and the cost of repair. When the inspection is completed, notify the tenants verbally and with a written notice.

Some time during the end of the tenancy, the landlord must give the tenant a written notice and explanation of why any or all of the deposit will not be returned. If it's $100 damage, deduct $100 from the rent deposit. Before refunding the rent deposit, make sure it coincides with your written notification of damage.

If all other criteria of moving out are satisfied, then the balance of the rent deposit can be used to pay part or all of the last month's rent. If all the terms of the termination of the lease are satisfied, the landlord must return the money within a 21-day period after the end of the lease.

Interest

Most states stipulate that the rent deposit must be returned with a certain amount of interest. Each state has different interest rates. Not paying that interest can be trouble you don't want.

In a case in Illinois court, the landlord didn't pay the required annual interest. The court awarded double the amount of the damages to the tenant and the landlord had to pay the tenant's attorney's fees. The interest money must be paid on the same date as the rent deposit is returned. The sad part of this scenario is that now there are some attorneys who prey on landlords even those who make innocent errors. Be careful.

Landlord's Rights

Believe it or not, there are some landlord's rights.

For instance, the tenant cannot use the security or rent deposit to insist that this money pay for rent or past-due rent until all other obligations of the terms are met. A lease is a legal contract. If a tenant breaks that lease, she can be held responsible for the remainder of the rent due under the terms of the lease.

If the case is taken to court, the tenant can be liable for a penalty. The burden, of course, is on the landlord. Before taking the case to court, the landlord must give the tenant a written notice that it is illegal to use the security deposit for the last rent payment. If that tenant should break the lease, it's best to end it all and find a new renter.

There are some state laws that specify that the landlord must make an attempt to find a tenant as soon as possible. When they say, "as soon as possible," I'm not at all that sure what they mean, but it would probably be a tough case to prove in court.

If and when a lease is broken by the tenant, make sure you keep specific records and details. If he calls and says he's moving because he's going to another town or another job, put that information in the record. You don't want to end up in court, defending yourself on the basis that the tenant has accused you of not taking care of the property adequately.

Do Not Confiscate Property for Past-Due Rent

The only way you, the owner of the property, can lock out a tenant or confiscate property for nonpayment of rent-past-due utilities and/or damage to the property is with a court order. Don't attempt to do it any other way. Tenants can and sometimes do file claims against landlords for almost any trumped-up incident, especially regarding rent deposits.

Unfortunately, there are times when the judge rules in favor of the tenant, and it's not unusual that in such cases the judge will awarded punitive damages and reasonable attorney's fees. Who knows how much that can be? Those are decisions made by a judge, and remember a judge is an attorney.

Dealing with Abandoned Personal Property

It's hard to find a tenant who hasn't left some personal property. That property can be anything from old clothing left in a closet, to davenports, mattresses, and beds, bedding, dressers, and knick-knacks. As I've researched information from landlords, they've told me that the number-one leftover personal property is a "dead" mattress.

Most abandoned property has little if any value, and it has to be removed from the premises. The only solution is calling the junk-garbage man or finding some method of burning whatever is left.

If you end up with property that you think has some value, that's a whole different story, and you want to protect yourself from any legal claim on the part of that tenant. Here's what you do.

Solution

Check the Law

First, by all means check with your respective state law covering abandoned property. Also make sure that you know whether you have a right to enter the property without notice. Most state laws specify that a landlord can enter the property if there's any sort of emergency such as fire or water damage, if there's reason to believe that the property is not maintained, if there are past-due obligations for heat and electricity, or if the premises are not adequately clean.

The following can also be considered acceptable: The tenant has moved out without proper notification and the landlord is forced to remove and store abandoned property. Once the property is stored, the tenant can request that it be returned, and then you the landlord have 24 hours to return the property if it's still in the rental unit, and if it's stored, 48 hours.

If that property hasn't been called for and it's totally abandoned, you, the landlord, have 60 days, at which time you may sell or get rid of the property. The landlord must give the tenant written notice by certified mail two weeks before making the sale.

From that money you can recover the costs of removing and storing the property, any back-due rent, and any damages the tenant has created on the property. Any leftover money (that'd be a miracle) must be returned to the tenant.

Again, here's protection for the tenant. You, the landlord may not hold any of the abandoned property and demand any rent or anything owed. If the tenant asks for the property back, and they owe for one or two or several month's rent, you have to return that property within 24 hours of demand by the tenant.

And here's the final blast. If the landlord doesn't return that property, that tenant can take the landlord to court, sue for damages the tenant suffered, plus reasonable attorneys fees and a penalty of (in Minnesota) $300. Eventually, if you can find the tenant you can charge for the moving and storage costs, but if this individual has been a questionable tenant, the odds of finding him are limited.

Dealing with an Abandoned Automobile

Contact the police or sheriff's office and tell them the circumstances. Of course, if it's a car owned by a former tenant, you should have all the information on the lease or rent application. This might entail doing some telephone work.

If it's not abandoned by a former tenant, then go to the police. I think I'd go there personally rather than by phone. When you do, bring as much information and details about the car as possible: the year, model, serial number, and, most important, the license plate number. The police can run the plate number through their computer and find the name and address of the titled owner. I'm sure they'll give you this information.

When you get this information, first try to make personal contact if you can find the person's phone number. If not, look in the telephone directory and try calling a relative or just pick out someone in the directory with the same last name and tell them you're trying to get in contact with so and so. Maybe, and I've seen it happen, they'll tell you, "No, but he's related to so and so."

If all that doesn't work, next try registered mail and a note on the envelope "FORWARD ADDRESS REQUESTED." Once you've run out of attempts of trying to get in touch with the individual, it's back to the police to report it as an abandoned vehicle. Ask them what procedure to take.

If the police confiscate the automobile, they can legally sell it without a title. It's called a "sheriff's sale" whereby the owner is given written notice. But here's what can happen. They will call a tow service, and from that point on there will be tow charges and storage charges that somebody is going to have to pay. It doesn't occur that often, but it does happen.

Chapter 17

The Positive Aspects of Real Estate Investing

Don't Be Discouraged

I hope this book has not discouraged anyone from becoming involved in real estate investing. This is basically a problem-solving book. I've probably dispensed some harsh negative facts and some pessimistic incidents regarding real estate investing. I've intentionally emphasized some of the various legal issues and troublesome events that can occur in the real estate and rental business. However, most of the problems I've outlined in this book are unusual and rarely occur. But remember, it only takes one negative incident or one lawsuit to break your spirit.

Real Estate Investing is a Positive

I want to assure you that real estate investing and the ownership of rental property is interesting, exhilarating, and a positive business. Real estate investing offers, without a doubt, a financial vehicle that gives the average person the ability to establish and build a net worth and accumulate enough wealth to acquire an estate nest egg. There aren't many businesses that give the average person this opportunity.

Probably one of the most positive aspects of investing in real estate is that it really doesn't take that much personal capital to purchase investment property. Some money, yes, but to realize an end result of increasing the value of your investment, it will take creativity, smart decisions, and dedicated work.

Motivation

It should be easy to motivate yourself to take good care of your property. You'll most likely be involved with hands-on work, both physical and mental labor. But what makes it exhilarating is the end result. You can stand there before your property and say, "That's mine."

One of the most exciting experiences of being involved with real estate is that when you take on a project and you begin working with buying more property or improving and renovating your property, it becomes easy to recognize the important fact that you're working for yourself.

There are no meetings to attend, no one dictating any moves you have to make, and no supervisor to answer to. You are the boss. What a wonderful feeling.

Positivism at Its Best

Over the years I've experienced a modicum of success in the real estate business. I've been asked, "You come from a humble background. What do you attribute your success to?" I can answer that. I've always associated myself with optimistic and positive-acting people. Most of my good friends, all who come from humble backgrounds such as mine, are successful in their endeavors. They include my friend, a self-made entrepreneur who started a small manufacturing company in his garage that eventually became a nationally recognized firm. Also, I include as one of my friends and business associates an attorney who is and always has been an upbeat, intelligent individual. And most importantly, he's honest. I've always respected his advice. And my good banker friend has always encouraged me to take some financial chances. They have all been a positive force in my life as well as my business career. Why am I telling you this story? Because I want to reinforce my theory that it pays to be surrounded by positive thinking and acting, and encouraging people.

How about Education?

In this business, education can be helpful but it's not all that necessary. You don't need an MBA degree from Harvard. You don't really need a college degree. But I want to add that a college education doesn't hurt.

In this business of real estate, and any business for that matter, I do believe it takes a little more than average intelligence, but you don't have to be a genius. I was fortunate and graduated from college. But I can assure you that I didn't gain my success because of my grade point average or my record of outstanding grades. I like to tell everyone that I graduated in the top 10 in my high school class." Of course, there were only 11 of us."

Here's another story about education, school, grades, and those sorts of things that I like to tell my friends and associates. "It looks to me like those students who got As and Bs, and those who were the valedictorians and salutatorians became school teachers, college professors, college and school administrators, and perhaps some doctors and most likely some attorneys. Those who got Cs, which includes me, became successful real estate investors."

I've probably told those two stories more times than I should have. But I've always liked them and thought they were rather humorous. However, it seems like some of my friends and associates don't agree and don't see the humor. In fact, some of them told me I was sick.

A Learning Experience

Most of my learning was on-the-job training. I read enough real estate books that helped build my confidence. To further your real estate education, read good books. Here are some good, positive real estate books that I think you'll like. I can recommend them because I've found them to be enlightening and interesting.

I especially favor the very first book I read about real estate investing, written by William Nickerson. That book has been out for many years and is still in print or at least in most libraries. It's titled *How I Turned $1,000 into $5 Million Dollars in Real Estate*, published by Simon and Schuster, New York. It's the book that got me started thinking positively about real estate and I said to myself, "That's something I can do."

The book *Landlording* by Leah Robinson is an extensive overview of real estate investing. I can assure you it can't be read in an evening. I consider this book a real estate encyclopedia.

Donald Trump's Book *How to Make a Deal* is a good real estate book. I think you'll enjoy and learn something by reading my recently published book, *The New No-Nonsense Landlord*, Revised and Expanded, published in 2003 by McGraw-Hill.

Thanks to Robert Bruss, an outstanding real estate expert, a syndicated columnist whose column appears in 300 newspapers all over the country, I've always received good reviews about my books. All the above named books were considered by Bruss as some of the top real estate books of all time.

Let me quote from Bruss's column, followed by his list of the 10 best real estate books:

> *When I talk with homebuyers and real estate investors, I am often asked to recommend the best real estate books. Since I read at least one realty book every two weeks, I see the best and worst books on my favorite topic. Today I would like to share the best books.*

With advance apologies to authors who wrote excellent books, which didn't make the list, here are the 10 best real estate books.

How I Turned $1,000 into $5 Million in Real Estate, BY William Nickerson, Simon and Schuster.

Nothing Down, By Robert G. Allen, Simon and Schuster

Trump: The Art of the Deal, By Donald Trump, Random House

The New No-Nonsense Landlord, By Richard H. Jorgensen, McGraw-Hill

The Realty Blue Book, By Robert De Heer, Professional Publishing Co.

Landlording, By Leigh Robinson, Express Publishing

How to Get Rich in Real Estate, By Robert W. Kent, Prentice-Hall

Invest in Debt, By Jim Napier, Inc, Jim Napier, Inc.

Aggressive Tax Avoidance for Real Estate Investors, By John T. Reed, Reed Publishing

Housewise, By Suzanne Brangham, Crown Publishers

This list dates back some years ago, but I trust the opinion of Robert Bruss, and I don't think you'll go wrong investing in any one or all of the above books. If Bruss says they're good, they're good.

The More You Read, the Better Your Future in This Business

I'm convinced that the more you read about this business, the more likely it is that it can and will be helpful in your business career. This book, *What Every Landlord Needs to Know*, and the others, should help you avoid some of the pitfalls of the business. If others before you made mistakes and miscalculations and they pass this experience on to you, you can then more easily avoid making the same errors, which sometimes can be costly mistakes.

It is my firm belief that after reading the good real estate books, if you end up with just one good idea from each book, that can help you become a more successful investor. Then it's all worth the effort.

It Helps to Be Type A

The following might not be the most important part of *What Every Landlord Needs to Know*, but at least it will give you something to think about, and I hope it can be a positive influence on your real estate life.

Let me first of all explain my interpretation of a Type A personality. I'll start by telling you that I am one. Being a Type A is not changeable. It's like saying your eyes are brown and you want to change them to blue. You can't. Nor can you basically change the characteristics of a Type A person. It's part of each individual's hereditary, physical, emotional, and mental makeup. Those of you reading this who are Type As, and I'd guess there are a lot of them because Type As and real estate are synonymous with one another, know what I mean?

The reason I bring this up in this book is because a Type A usually will spend a great deal of time and energy and make it a continuous struggle to accomplish or to accumulate things, such as property, wealth, or whatever the goal is. That means a Type A will usually be an aggressive real estate investor.

Let me explain further. A Type A person is the kind who must have something going on all the time, some kind of physical or mental activity that occupies her mind and body. It's difficult for a Type A person to just sit and do nothing. If there's nothing going on, a Type A will make up something. If the event of the moment is boring, often a Type A will start another project and do two projects simultaneously. And a Type A is always urgently on the go. He doesn't understand the word "tranquillity."

That alone makes for a qualified real estate investor. Type As cannot tolerate people who do stupid things. That's why I've said to be in the real estate investment business you should be somewhat sharper and have better-than-average intelligence.

The fact is most Type As intellectually are above average. Some become overachievers. Usually overachievers gain more victories than defeats in their goals.

As far as I can tell from my experience with real estate investments, I've always experienced many more victories than defeats. Type As can usually be counted on to get things done. They, for the most part, are the movers and shakers. And it takes a mover and shaker to carry on a successful real estate investment business.

Here's something else. A Type A is one who watches and criticizes other drivers and will talk to the other driver through the windshield, knowing full well that the other driver can't hear a word being said. Type As are especially impatient and upset with drivers who pay no attention to what they're doing.

For the real estate investor, that means they can't sit around and wait for others to do what's supposed to be done. Having to do with real estate, this includes service people and bureaucracies. Being a Type A creates a great deal of anxiety and stress on the body, and sometimes Type A's will burn themselves out.

Chapter 18

Forms

RENTAL APPLICATION

Date_____

Insert a blank line here

Property Address_____ Apt. No_____

Beginning Date_____ Terminating Date_____

Total Rent Amount Per Month_____

All Amounts Due Must Be Paid Prior to Occupancy

Payment Schedule:

Security Deposit_____   Date_____

Credit Check_____   Date_____

Rent Paid_____   Date_____

Pet Deposit_____   Date_____

Other_____   Date_____

Applicant's Name_____ Age_____

Social Security Number _____

Spouse's Name_____ Age_____

Social Security Number _____

Children_____ Ages_____

Present Landlord_____

Address _____

Rented From_____ To_____

Previous Landlord _____

Address _____

Rented From_____ To_____

Employer _____

Address_____ Phone_____

Number of Years_____Position_____Salary_____

Spouse's Employer _____

Address_____ Phone_____

Number of Years_____Position_____Salary_____

References

_____ Phone_____

_____ Phone_____

Bank _____

Address_____ Phone_____

Have you been convicted of any crimes?_____ Date_____

Violation _____

Have you ever filed for bankruptcy?_____ Date_____

Do you have any present or past judgments? _____

Explain _____

Applicants hereby authorize the owner, manager, association, or agent, to obtain a credit report from any credit reporting agency and to interview third parties, such as business associates, financial sources, family members, friends, and/or neighbors.

The signed applicant hereby certifies that the answers given herein are true and correct. Applicant understands that any false statement made here will be sufficient grounds for refusal to rent, eviction, and loss of any security deposit.

Signature_____ Date_____

Signature_____ Date_____

Management Signature_____ Date_____

LEASE AND CONTRACTUAL AGREEMENT

Date_____

Property Owner or Manager _____
Address and Phone Number _____

Property Address_____ Apt. No_____
Beginning Date_____ Terminating Date_____
Length of Lease _____

Payment Schedule:
Security Deposit_____ Date_____
Service Charge_____ Date_____
Other Charges_____ Date_____
Utilities Included: Heat_____ Electricity_____ Cable_____
Utilities Paid by Tenant: Heat_____ Electricty_____ Cable_____

Lease Holder's Name: (List all persons, including children and date of birth who will reside in rental unit.)

_____

_____

_____

_____

Management

_____

By_____
Date_____

Resident _____

_____

_____

Date_____

TERMS OF LEASE:

Rent: Resident will pay full month's rent before midnight on the first day of each month. Each above-signed resident is responsible for paying the full amount due. Upon eviction all signed residents are responsible for full monthly rent and if not the following late charges are applicable:

_____$20.00 late rent payment
_____$20.00 eviction penalty
_____$20.00 returned check

Occupancy: Only signed residents may occupy the premises. Any change must be approved by management. Single lease holder must give notice when and if subletting the apartment or unit.

Occupant will not misuse or damage any part of the properties, will not paint without consent, and will keep the unit clean.

When vacating, occupant will leave the unit in good condition, exception being normal wear and tear.

Occupant responsibilities: The tenant shall be responsible for maintenance and repairs of inside fixtures that are not main lines. This includes plugged drains in kitchen, bathroom sinks, shower and toilets, broken windows, damaged appliances, damaged carpets, window coverings, and generally all leased property that becomes damaged or nonworking during the term of the lease. This does not cover normal wear and tear to the property.

Tenant agrees to immediately report all damages to any part of the rental property, both inside and out.

Tenant agrees to pay for all damages to property caused by occupants; this includes the house or apartment and the outside yard or common area. The tenant will hire necessary service to make repairs at the tenant's expense.

Security Deposit: The owner-manager will keep all or part of the security deposit for damage to the apartment beyond natural wear and tear and for rent and other money owed.

Eviction Notice: The following violations qualify the owner-manager to serve eviction notice:

> Loud and/or boisterous activities or parties.
> Thoughtless disturbance infringing on rights of other residents.
> Using the property for any illegal or dangerous activities.
> Illegal drug activities of any kind.
> Prostitution.
> Illegal firearms in possession.
> Stolen property on the premises.
> False application.

If at any time management suspects any of the above, management has the right to enter the rental unit for inspection.

If rent is paid, this does not disqualify management from proceeding with eviction notice for any violation of the lease.

If management brings legal action against occupant/occupants, those occupants must pay management's attorney and legal fees and any other expenses incurred. This will include paying a collection agency to recover past-due rent.

Pets: No animals or pets are allowed without consent of owner-management.

Duration of Lease: If management is unable to provide occupancy at the start of the lease, the occupant-lease holder cannot sue the management for any resulting damage.

Liability: Owner/management is not responsible for damage or injury done to resident or guests that was not caused by owner/management.

The owner/management is to carry insurance for fire damage to the building. However, the owner/management will not provide insurance for tenant's personal property and furnishings.

Management recommends that resident/occupant retain renter's insurance to cover personal property and furnishings and to protect against injuries or property damage.

Resident shall pay for any loss from property damage or cost of repair or service caused by negligence or improper use.

Resident shall pay owner/management for any disposable property in the amount of $25 each.

Other Stipulations:

_____

_____

_____

Management Responsibilities: The owner/management of the property will maintain reasonable and proper repair except when damage is caused by the resident or guest. Management/owner will keep the property in accordance with health and safety codes. Management/owner will maintain all common areas and keep these areas reasonably clean and in good condition. Management is responsible for all systems, such as roofs, heating-cooling, electrical, plumbing (main lines) and the operation of these systems.

DISCLOSURE OF INFORMATION ON LEAD-BASED PAINT AND LEAD-BASED HAZARDS

Lead-Based HazardousWarning: (42 U.S.C. 4852(d) Most housing built prior to 1978 may contain lead-based paint, paint chips, and dust that can pose health hazards if not taken care of properly. Lead exposure can be especially hazardous to young children and pregnant women.

Landlords must disclose the presence of known lead-based paint in the dwelling and provide to the tenants a federally approved pamphlet on lead poisoning prevention.

Manager-Owner's Disclosure:

Mark answer with Yes or No:

Known lead-based paint and/or hazards are present in housing _____

Management has no knowledge of lead-based paint or hazards _____

Management-owner has provided records pertaining
to lead-based hazards in the housing   _____

Resident has received copies of above information   _____

Resident has received pamphlet
Protect Your Family from Lead in your Home   _____

The above information has been provided to the resident and is accurate to the best of their knowledge.

Management Owner_____ Date _____

Resident_____ Date _____

GUIDE TO MOVING IN

<u>**Your Company Name**</u>
Address
Phone Number
Manager

Tenant's Responsibilities:

1. Rent must be paid on or before the first of each month at the above address.

2. All tenants are responsible for utilities, including electric, gas (if applicable), TV, and computer cable and phone.

3. Only those named in the lease can occupy the apartment. Guests are to stay no more than three days.

4. No pets.

5. Use sewing needles or small nails for pictures or posters on walls.

6. In a private home you are responsible for mowing lawn and snow removal.

7. Do not flush tampons or condoms into toilets and through the sewer line.

8. Check smoke detectors and fire extinguishers once a month.

9. No waterbeds.

10. Protect your personal property and cover your liability exposure with sufficient renter's insurance.

MOVING-OUT GUIDELINES

The following is a list of obligations to adhere to when moving out:

1. Contact phone, cable, electrical, gas, and post office with your new address and notify each that you will cease using their services at the end of your lease.
2. You are responsible for all utilities until the end of the month, not the day you move out. Make sure all obligations with these utilities are paid in full.
3. Clean
      Stove, oven, under burners
      Refrigerator
      Cabinets
      Sinks
      Floors
      Bathroom
      Toilets
      Windows
      Closets
      Carpets (If necessary we will have carpet cleaned and deducted from your deposit.)
4. Remove all garbage.
5. Set up time for inspection.
6. Leave forwarding address and refund will be mailed to you within legal period of time.
7. Move out time is 12:00 noon. There is an hourly fee charge if move is made after the noon deadline.

MOVING-OUT LETTER

YOUR BUSINESS NAME
PHONE NUMBER
ADDRESS

Dear (Tenant)

We have received notice that you will be leaving your rental unit. This is to let you know that your tenancy will end at 12:00 noon on _____.
It is imperative that you are moved out by noon of the last day of the month. There will be a charge for time you occupy the premises after the noon deadline.

Following is a list of informational items.

We will be showing your apartment to potential applicants. We will contact you when we have a showing scheduled if possible. If you aren't available, we will attempt to contact you at work and make arrangements for the showing, especially if the new tenant is from out of our community.

Please keep your unit comparatively clean as we wish to make a good impression on the new potential tenant.

Please observe the MOVE-OUT GUIDELINE. Make sure your apartment is clean. If we have to pay for cleaning service, this will be deducted from your rent deposit. Also make sure garbage has been removed and the keys have been returned.

We appreciate the fact that you've been a good tenant. If the apartment has not been rented by the time you move out, if you have a responsible friend who would like to rent the unit we will add an addition $25 to your deposit refund.

Sincerely,

CRIME-FREE, DRUG-FREE ADDENDUM FOR HOUSING

Crime-Free/Drug-Free Housing: Any and all of the following activities are illegal and disqualify anyone from occupying any crime-free, drug-free housing. Anyone involved in any form of drug activities is subject to immediate eviction from the premises, which includes the following: Manufacturing, distributing, purchasing, using or possession with intent to manufacture, sell, distribute, or use of a controlled substance, or possession of drug paraphernalia, as defined in Section 102 of the Controlled Substance act. This also includes any illegal activity such as prostitution, harboring stolen goods, and illegally possessing guns.

Resident's Responsibility:

1. The resident and/or occupant of the premises, or any members of the resident's household or a guest or other person under the resident's control shall not engage in illegal activity, including drug-related illegal manufacture, sale, distribution, purchase, use or possession with intent to manufacture, sell, distribute, or use of a controlled substance, or possession of drug paraphernalia.

2. The resident, and/or any member of the resident's household or a guest or other person under the resident's control shall not engage in any act intended to facilitate illegal activity, including drug-related illegal activity on or near the premises.

3. Resident or members of the household will not permit the dwelling to be used for, or to facilitate, any illegal activity.

4. Residents or members of the household or guests or any other person under the resident's control shall not engage in acts of violence or threats of violence, including, but not limited to, the unlawful discharge of firearms, prostitution, criminal street gang activity, intimidation, or any other breach of the rental agreement that otherwise jeopardizes the health, safety, or welfare of the landlord.

5. Violation of any of the above provisions shall be a material violation of the lease and cause for termination of occupancy. A single violation of any of these provisions of this addendum shall be deemed a serious violation and noncompliance with the lease.

6. It is understood and agreed that a single violation shall be good cause for termination of this lease. Proof of violation shall not require criminal conviction but shall be by the preponderance of the evidence.

7. This addendum is incorporated into the lease executed by the owner and resident and shall govern.

MANAGEMENT   RESIDENT

_____   _____

_____   _____

Dated_____   Dated_____

Index

About the Author

Richard H. Jorgensen has been a landlord, entrepreneur, and real estate developer for more than 30 years.